"*Tools for Teaching* is the perfect book for any catechist who has ever cried, "Help!" For it is chock-full of help—the solid, practical kind of help all catechists (from rookies to veterans) can really use. Paprocki gives tips for everything from writing good lesson plans and maintaining discipline to preparing for when things go wrong and knowing when and how to break. As I read the book, I found myself saying things like 'Yes!' 'Right On!' 'How Clever!' 'Why didn't I think of that?' 'Wow!' Though I found all the sections of the chapters helpful, I especially liked the catechist's quote and the prayer at the end of each chapter."

Melannie Svoboda, SND
Author, *Peeling Back Eggshells* and
Traits of a Healthy Spirituality

"I have read and enjoyed Joseph Paprocki's *Tools for Teaching*. This book is filled with the wisdom and practical advice that comes from being in the trenches. The suggestions are tried and true.

"The book is organized and easy to read. The analogy of home repairs—when to attempt things on your own and when to seek the pros—is carried through the entire book. The important words and the catechetical do's and don'ts are easy to spot and to remember. I especially enjoyed the spotlight example. Learning when to keep the spotlight and when (and how) to shift the spotlight to students is something that is helpful to new catechists as well as to those who are veterans. DREs and those responsible for catechist training will find useful ide⸱ ⸱d tools."

Bar⸱
Teach⸱

"*Tools for Teaching* is a godsend for beginnir⸱ echists who wish to polish their classr⸱ ⸱ gy of home improvement, it instruct⸱ ⸱ up God's kingdom. As a result, the manual ⸱ ⸱d entertaining. Best of all, it equips catechists wit⸱ ⸱or preventing and for dealing with problems thr⸱ ⸱ections called Troubleshooting, Catechetical Do's and Don'ts, and Warning!"

Kathleen Glavich, SND
General Editor of the *Christ Our Life* series (Loyola Press)
Author, *Discipline Made Easy*

"This book is written in a clear and positive style. It is filled with anecdotes that educate and entertain. It would be a welcome addition to any parish's religious education library."

Peggy Weber
Springfield Catholic Observer

"The book has the look and feel of a home improvement book, including chapters such as 'A Do-It-Yourself Approach to Improving Your Catechetical Skills,' 'The Extension Cord: Plugging into the Power of Prayer' and 'Sandpaper: Smooothing Out Discipline Problems.' Included in each of the chapters are sections on 'Warnings,' 'Trouble-shooting,' 'Dos and Don'ts,' 'The Catechist's Quote' and 'A Prayer for the Catechist.'"

Bill Britt
The New World, Chicago

"Paprocki isn't a carpenter, painter, electrician, or roofer. He is a catechetical consultant at the Chicago Archdiocesan Office for Religious Education. Concentrating on preparation and instruction, his book offers realistic answers to some common problems."

Jill M. Caravan
A.D. Times

"Here is a do-it-yourself manual that offers step-by-step instruction for approaching a wide variety of catechetical challenges: planning lessons, handling discipline problems, using textbooks and teacher manuals, praying with your class, choosing appropriate student activities and much more."

Theology Book Service

"This book is designed for people who find themselves in teaching situations with little actual teaching experience. Joe Paprocki offers practical suggestions on how to cope with the physical demands of the new catechetical role, and only thereafter to find one's own teaching style."

Paul Mathew St. Pierre
The British Columbia Catholic

TOOLS
for Teaching

Classroom Tips
for Catechists

Joe Paprocki

TWENTY-THIRD PUBLICATIONS
Mystic, CT 06355

Acknowledgments

I would like to thank the staff and parishioners of St. Mary of the Assumption Parish in Chicago for encouraging me to share my gifts and to the catechists of St. Mary's for putting up with my "tool time" tips.

Thanks to all the catechists who shared their wisdom in the "Catechist Quote" sections of each chapter.

Special thanks to the people at Twenty-Third Publications for inviting me to undertake such an enjoyable project!

Second Printing 1998

Twenty-Third Publications
185 Willow Street
P.O. Box 180
Mystic, CT 06355
(860) 536-2611
(800) 321-0411

ISBN 0-89622-726-X
Library of Congress Catalog Card Number 97-60103
Printed in the U.S.A.

Dedication

To Jo, Mike, and Amy,
whose love has brought immeasurable
"home improvement" to my life.
And to Connie Wilkinson
for guiding many young
"apprentices" to The Way

Tools for Teaching

Introduction

A Do-It-Yourself Approach to Improving Your Catechetical Skills

Imagine that you are moving into a new home or apartment. There's a great deal of work to be done, isn't there? Aside from moving all of your personal belongings and furniture, you find that there are many repairs and improvements to be accomplished before you can move in one piece of anything! A leaky faucet, a loose hinge, a room that needs wallpapering, some faulty wiring, etc. Sound familiar? Most of us have experienced this challenge: how do we accomplish all of the repairs that need to be done before we move in? If we call professionals to fix everything, it may take longer than we hope and cost too much. If we try to do it ourselves, we may end up making more of a mess than anything. If you're anything like me, you compromise: some of the work gets done by professionals while the majority of it is accomplished by way of the do-it-yourself method.

The Do-it-Yourself Method

At one time or another, all of us have tried to undertake some home repairs by ourselves. We go to the local bookstore, video store, or hardware store where numerous home improvement manuals and videos provide step-by-step instructions for do-it-yourself repairs. These manuals are very helpful in allowing the novice to tackle some projects that would require much more time and money if handled by a professional. By following the step-by-step instructions, we are able to do some minor plumbing, electrical work, and even construction! These accomplishments, however, are no reason to give up our day jobs. Just because we conquer one or two minor do-it-yourself projects does not mean that we are now able to advertise our services as a professional plumber, electrician, or construction worker. To be certified in these fields takes a great deal of time, experience, study, and preparation. Sometimes the do-it-yourself method works. Other times it fails. The bottom line is that we need both: professional help and the guidance of a do-it-yourself manual.

The Do-It-Yourself Catechist?

Is there such a thing as a do-it-yourself catechist? It is true that, as catechists, many of us find ourselves face-to-face with challenges for which we have had no formal training. What are we to do? Do we tell the children to wait until we complete our formal training? Do we run to the professional (the DRE or master catechist) every time a problem arises? Or, do we learn to handle these problems by ourselves? The answer is a combination of all of the above.

For the most part, we will have to discover on our own how to handle certain situations and challenges. Like a home improvement manual, *Tools for Teaching* is a do-it-yourself manual to assist you, the catechist, in handling these challenges until you receive formal training and certification. In the short run, the do-it-yourself method of teaching catechism will get you through some real challenges. In the long run, however, it is crucial for you to complete formal training and certification as a catechist. Think about it: those entrusted with fixing pipes must study for five years before becoming a licensed plumber; those entrusted with repairing electrical wires must complete ten thousand hours of training before being certified as a union electrician. It makes sense that catechists, people who are entrusted with the spiritual formation of children, *must* complete formal training and formation leading to certification as a catechist. *Tools for Teaching* is not meant to be a substitute for formal catechetical formation and training. Rather, it is meant to be an aide to catechists for handling immediate challenges as well as a catalyst for preparing catechists to attend and participate in formal catechetical formation.

In the Meantime...

Someday, you will accomplish the catechist certification process that is required by your parish, cluster of parishes, or diocese. In the meantime, however, you've got classes happening—now! *Tools for Teaching* is what you need to tackle those challenges that you are currently facing. Think of it as a home improvement manual that will provide you with step-by-step instructions for approaching a wide variety of catechetical challenges. You will one day receive formal training, in the meantime, do it yourself!

Chapter One

The Blueprint: The Importance of Lesson Planning

Are you like me? When you try to assemble a piece of furniture or a toy, do you try to do so without looking at the instructions? I admit that this is one of my worst habits. Inevitably, I get three-quarters of the way done and find a screw or a bolt that I was supposed to use in step one! Once, I tried to put together a shiny new tricycle for my daughter as a surprise for her birthday. I assembled the whole thing, only to find a very large bolt lying next to my foot. For the life of me, I was unable to figure out where it was supposed to go. Then and only then did I pull out the instructions. Much to my dismay, I had left out a very important bolt that literally held the whole tricycle together. I suppose this is why we should read the instructions first!

Can you imagine a builder attempting to construct a house without first looking at the blueprints? What a catastrophe that would be! The blueprints hold the key to constructing something properly. Without them, we run the risk of an eventual collapse of the whole structure. Obviously, we would never think of building a house without first looking over the blueprints. Yet, when it comes to teaching a lesson, we are often tempted to forge ahead without the proper amount of planning. If we are going to build a foundation of faith for the children we teach, we need to read the blueprints.

Planning Good Lessons
Spontaneity is nice, but those who are best at spontaneity have

done their homework and are well prepared for whatever may come their way. As a catechist, you need to search for the proper balance between spontaneity and rigidity. Lesson planning is the way the competent catechist looks over the blueprints for the upcoming lesson and prepares for building a sound structure.

As a student teacher, I was taught that lesson planning was seventy percent of the art of teaching. Now, there may be no way to scientifically prove that, but after nine years of teaching high-school religion, I have found it to be absolutely true. Solid, detailed lesson planning helps the catechist to function in the most effective manner possible, while preempting a large variety of discipline problems. A good lesson planner is one who imagines every possible scenario and prepares for it. A good lesson planner is one who examines the blueprint for the lesson, knows how it is to be built, and proceeds to build it effectively.

Tips for Lesson Planning

1. *Look ahead.* First and foremost, know your calendar! The lesson you are planning is only part of a larger plan for the whole year. If you were in charge of a construction job, you would need to know how one step builds upon another until the structure is complete. In your lesson planning, you need to get a picture of the whole calendar year and see how much time you have to accomplish your goals. Get a good feel for how this lesson can build off of the previous one and lay the foundation for the next.

2. *Get to know your text and your class.* While no text is the be-all and end-all of teaching, your text *is* a primary resource at your fingertips. Get to know its strengths and weaknesses ahead of time. Get a sense of the whole book and then zero in on a set of chapters or a unit to see how the next lesson fits in with the whole. At the same time, get to know your class and how capable they are of handling the text as it is written. Your DRE has more than likely made an excellent selection but that does not rule out the possibility that a certain chapter or section is beyond or below your class's capabilities.

3. *Examine the teacher notes in the instructor's manual.* Instructor's manuals are often a catechist's best friend. Most

of the popular texts used in religious education classes today have excellent instructor's manuals that lay out the lesson much like a blueprint and offer step-by-step instructions. The more you know about the teacher notes, the better you will be able to implement your lesson and still leave room for spontaneity.

4. *Visualize yourself teaching the lesson.* A highly effective teaching tool is visualization, the practice of using your imagination to experience specific situations in hopes of learning behaviors that can be incorporated into your real life repertoire. Good lesson planning involves visualizing yourself teaching the class. Imagine every possible scenario and how you would react. Keep a notepad nearby to jot down important thoughts or ideas that will now become part of your lesson. Write down a list of materials that you will need to enhance certain situations. Imagine problems that might arise and visualize how you would best handle them. With this visualization complete, you will feel as though you've already taught this lesson once and are now building upon it.

5. *Make adjustments to fit your particular class.* No lesson plan is ironclad. Once you've picked up the gist of the lesson, think of your particular class's readiness (or lack thereof) for what your lesson calls for and make the necessary adjustments. You may have a class that is not very talkative while the lesson calls for discussion. Perhaps you will need to make an adjustment and allow for some nonverbal form of expression. Whatever the case, the better you know your class, the better you'll be able to make adjustments so that their lesson will be as effective as possible.

6. *Know your goals and learning outcomes (objectives).* It is crucial that you know what the purpose of your lesson is. Don't settle for "my goal is to cover chapter four." Like a contractor reading a blueprint, you need to know whether you are building a town house or a condominium! Goals and learning outcomes (sometimes referred to as objectives) are statements you include in your lesson plan that state concretely and in measurable terms, what it is you hope to

accomplish. Without goals and objectives, you will never know if you've accomplished what you have set out to do.

7. *Get your materials ready.* Before you go into the classroom, be sure you have all of the materials you will need to complete the lesson properly. There's nothing worse than reaching a point in the lesson when you tell children to cut pictures out of magazines only to find out that you don't have scissors (or magazines!). Your DRE will be most helpful in this area, but a competent catechist does not wait until the last moment to ask for such materials. Your visualization of your lesson will help you to see what materials you will need that perhaps were not listed in the instructor's manual.

8. *Have Plan B ready.* Part of your visualization of this lesson may include the possibility that what you're hoping to accomplish may not work! Always have an option ready in case something falls flat or just isn't working the way you had hoped.

Warning!
Without proper lesson planning, you are vulnerable to boredom, poor discipline, lackluster performance, and poor participation.

Words to Remember

Goals: A goal is a general statement of direction for the lesson. It is a broad statement and is not always measurable. It is a guiding statement for the lesson or unit. Example: children will develop an appreciation for the Letters from Christian Scripture.

Learning outcomes: A learning outcome (or objective) is a more concise statement of expected performance or behavior stated in concrete terms. Example: children will identify four major components of a Letter from Christian Scripture and will compose a contemporary letter using those four components.

Instructor's manual: Accompanying any student text should be a manual prepared for the instructor providing background on the lesson as well as step-by-step suggestions for implementing the lesson. If you have not received an instructor's manual, talk to your DRE or contact the publisher of the textbook.

Troubleshooting

If you don't have and are unable to acquire a teacher's manual, thoroughly read through the text and develop your own goals and objectives before writing out a step-by-step plan for your lesson. If you are not happy with your first attempt at a lesson plan, do not abandon it. Be patient. Be prepared to switch gears but don't do so too quickly. If you are coming up blank, take a break, come back to it, and don't hesitate to ask others for help.

Catechetical Dos and Don'ts

Do...
•overplan
•be creative
•be thorough
•consult other resources

Don't...
•get lazy
•get careless
•be rigid
•assume the publisher's lesson plan will work

Catechist Quote

"When I was in the classroom, I measured the success of my planning by how many students asked to go to the washroom! If no one asked to be excused, I knew I had them in the palm of my hand. If I had several washroom requests, I knew it was time to change my course of action! Perhaps it was time to have the children gather on the floor around me for a Bible story or a personal story of how this lesson affects my life. In your lesson planning, try to alternate between quiet time and activity throughout the lesson. The more that you put into your lesson planning, the more you and your students will get out of the lesson. I tell my teachers to say a little prayer knowing that God will guide their way through both the planning and the actual teaching of the lesson."

—Janet Schneider
(DRE/Former Preschool through Grade Five Catechist)

A Prayer for Catechists

Lord Jesus, Rabbi and Teacher, you said that the foolish person built a foundation on sand while the wise person built upon solid rock. Help me to build my classes upon the solid rock foundation of good lesson planning so that when the wind comes and the rains buffet, my class will withstand the pressures and the children will come to know that Your Word will endure all things, for you are Lord forever and ever. Amen.

Chapter Two

The Tape Measure: Choosing Activities that Fit

My wife and I have a habit of purchasing things that don't fit in our house. On one occasion, we found two adorable love seats that we thought would turn an empty bedroom into a family room. In the store, they looked so small. Of course, when they were delivered, they suddenly looked humongous. They barely fit through the doorway. On another occasion, we put together a new entertainment center and then went out to buy a new TV. Our eyes got a little big and we ended up bringing home a twenty-seven-inch TV. You guessed it...too big! Luckily we were able to return it and buy a smaller screen that fit. You can be sure that the first item on my Christmas list that coming year was a tape measure. We learned our lesson: before we go out to buy any type of furniture, we now do what we should have done all along—measure to see if it will fit.

Choosing Activities that Fit Your Goals

As part of your lesson planning, you will ultimately determine an action plan, a format in which your lesson will be experienced. A few possibilities are lecture, role plays, debate, poster work, group work discussion, guest speaker, read text, quiz game, and meditation.

How do you know which one to pick? Will the method of class activity you have chosen fit with your goals and learning outcomes? Like buying a piece of furniture or constructing something, you need to measure and determine if the activity you

—————————— **10** ——————————

have chosen is a good fit both for your lesson and for your particular class. You certainly wouldn't choose to lecture if the goal was to experience God in the silence of solitude! That may seem obvious, but for each class we teach, we need to not only alter our activities for variety but also to make sure that what we have chosen is the best vehicle for achieving our goals. Likewise, we need to be sure that what we have chosen is appropriate for the particular age group we are teaching.

I recall once being asked to do a presentation on sexuality for junior-high students (who I assumed would be seventh and eighth graders). I decided to put together a video of how TV portrays sexuality. The resulting images from MTV, soap operas, dramas, and sitcoms were quite fascinating. However, when I arrived for the presentation, I realized too late that junior high for this program meant sixth graders. Needless to say, they were far too immature to articulate any reaction about the video images and their portrayal of sexuality. It made for a very uncomfortable experience and it was my fault for not measuring ahead of time to see if the activity would fit.

Tips for Choosing Your Activities

1. *Review your goals and learning outcomes.* If you know your goals and learning outcomes well, quite often they will give you a clue as to what type of activity you should choose. If the goals and learning outcomes call for the children to express or articulate an understanding of a certain topic, then you know you need to do something more than lecture. If the lesson calls for an understanding of community, it should be obvious to you that some type of group work would be appropriate. Common sense will often dictate what vehicle you choose. If you plan to vacation in Hawaii, you more than likely must select an airline or cruise ship—an automobile or train will do little good!

2. *Review the age, gender, spiritual maturity of your class.* Avoid the mistake I made in not checking out carefully the age group to whom I was to give a presentation on sexuality. Picture your class and the individuals in it and imagine yourself delivering the lesson you've planned. Be careful to avoid

the temptation of bringing in some idea straight from an adult religious education experience you've had without first adapting it to make it more age-appropriate.

3. *Consult a list of possible teaching formats.* If you have to drill a hole, you have a whole range of different size drill bits and screws to choose from. As a catechist, you also have a wide range and variety of activities from which to select. Don't get caught in a rut of doing the same thing every time you teach. In the next chapter, we will provide a list of various teaching formats and discuss what is involved in making each one work properly.

4. *Select an appropriate activity and see if it fits.* Once you select what type of activity you are going to use, place it into your lesson plan and see if it connects with your introduction and conclusion. As part of your visualization, imagine the activity unfolding and determine whether it will be appropriate and workable. Ask yourself if this activity achieves the goals and learning outcomes you have set for this lesson. If you decide to go with it, be sure you are prepared with all of the materials you may need.

5. *Employ praxis.* Praxis refers to the connection between theory and practice. It is one thing to have an idea, theory, or concept to pass on to someone else. It is entirely another thing to engage an individual or class in the *experience* of that idea or concept. In most teaching texts, you will find three parts to a lesson: examining the life experience of the student; introducing the idea, theory, or concept to be taught (Christian Tradition); integrating the two.

   As you plan out your lesson, you will need to identify proper activities that will invite your students to relate/articulate their life experience, communicate the gospel message, and somehow make a connection between the gospel message and their life experience. Unless the gospel connects to real life, it will be like a seed that has not taken root. By using the proper methods and activities, you achieve good praxis or integration of theory and experience.

6. *Select an alternate activity.* As always, be prepared to bail out if need be. If your selected activity is failing or just doesn't

fit, be prepared with another as a backup. A good example of this is the catechist who is all set to show a video only to discover that the VCR doesn't work or couldn't be obtained that particular day or period. Always be ready to move on to an alternate plan of action.

 Warning!
If you do not select activities that fit your goals and your class, you set yourself up for monotony, boredom, and possible failure. If you do not alter your activities, the children will lose interest. As a catechist, you are not called upon to be an entertainer, but, by the same token, you cannot assume that reading from the text and lecturing will achieve an appreciation for the Word of God.

Words to Remember

Pedagogy: Refers to the art of teaching, especially in relation to teaching methods. A catechist who has good pedagogy is one who understands the various methods available and utilizes them well.

Methodology: Refers to an orderly arrangement of things. A competent catechist employs the proper methodology or orderly arrangement of the lesson in order to achieve the goals and learning outcomes set forth.

Action Plan: A lesson plan is much more detailed than simply deciding to cover chapter five! A catechist needs an action plan, or a step-by-step plan for moving through the lesson, employing a variety of methods and activities.

Praxis: Refers to the *integration* of theory and practice. In order for an idea or concept to truly be incorporated into the life of a person, it needs to be connected to real life experience.

Troubleshooting

If you find yourself in a teaching rut, consult a list of various teaching activities (as found in next chapter) and try some on for size. You may be suffering from a simple case of monotony. If an activity you have chosen is not working or is inappropriate, examine why: look at the age-appropriateness of your selection and examine the spiritual and emotional maturity of your class. Employing a variety of activities in your lessons requires more preparation but results in better classes, a more relaxed catechist, better discipline, and more spontaneity.

Catechetical Dos and Don'ts

Do...
- be creative and innovative
- be versatile
- be daring
- prepare carefully
- observe others teach

Don't...
- be an entertainer
- be gimmicky
- impose inappropriate activities
- wing it
- select activities just because *you* like them

Catechist Quote

"Sometimes things happen in class that you are totally unprepared for—God's little surprises! I have been a catechist at the junior high, high school, and elementary levels for almost twenty years. I feel that it has been very helpful to me to be prepared, flexible, creative, and understanding. I try to make sure activities fit by listening to, discussing with, and encouraging my students. Most importantly, before class begins, I set a few minutes aside to put myself in God's presence and become God's instrument. In this way, I know that God is working through me and will make things fit. There is nothing more exciting than to experience our young people experiencing God in their lives!"

—John Maier (Junior High)

A Prayer for Catechists

Jesus, sometimes you told stories, other times you performed miracles. Sometimes you spoke for long stretches, other times you said very little. Sometimes you used images and metaphors, other times you spoke quite directly. You seemed to know what was right for the appropriate people at the appropriate time. Help me to choose the best way to bring your Word to life for the children I teach so that glory may be given to your name. Amen.

Chapter Three

Color Charts:
Selecting Student Activities

One of the more fun things about painting a room is looking over all of the color charts and the countless varieties of colors from which to choose. You can select anything from apricot beige to sunlight peach or rose pink to imperial purple. Of course, you can always stick with a basic white or, if you are slightly adventurous, perhaps an off-white. But how drab! Today, with the thousands of colors available through computer technology, painting a room can be a real exercise in creative expression.

Student Activities

The same holds true of student activities. All too often, catechists find themselves locked into the same old color scheme when it comes to classroom activities: there's your basic white (reading from the text) and your off-white (the catechist speaking about the text). A catechist needs to realize that there are literally hundreds of varieties of student activities available to add color and excitement to any lesson. Like an imaginative home decorator using a color chart, the catechist needs to look over the possibilities and ask what would be most appropriate. While hot pink may be your favorite color, it may not be the best color to paint your teenaged son's bedroom. By the same token, while there are a variety of wonderful activities to choose for your classes, you need to be sure the activity fits your class and your goals/objectives for the lesson.

Tips for Choosing Student Activities

1. *Become thoroughly familiar with the various student activities available to you.* In this chapter, you will find an extensive list of student activities—get to know them well before using them.

2. *View these activities in action.* If at all possible, make arrangements to observe another catechist or an actual classroom teacher to see someone use a student activity that you are interested in implementing.

3. *Review the goals and learning outcomes of your lesson.* Determine if you have selected the appropriate student activity for your class.

4. *Keep all of the materials you need for each particular student activity well organized and in an accessible place.* This way, when you decide to use that activity for your lesson, you will have it at your fingertips.

Warning!

—Keep the materials for your collection of student activities organized. Be sure that your student activity materials are out of the reach of children, who can lose and confuse important materials.

—Select student activities that are appropriate for your lessons and your students. Games or activities that work well for primary age students may blow up in your face if you try them with junior high students.

—Be sure you know what you are selecting. I've selected student activities I thought would work only to find out they don't work the way the directions suggested. Don't just pull out any student activity just for the sake of having something to do. Be sure you know what the activity is for and how it is to be implemented.

Words to Remember

Unlike other chapters, this glossary is somewhat extensive, covering a wide range of student activities, an explanation of what is involved, and what the purpose of the activity may be.

Texts: Texts are an undeniably valuable resource filled with excellent information. However, it is important to remember that it is only a resource and should not be the only way of accessing information. When reading text, break it down into sections keeping in mind the attention span of your students. Break away from the text for discussion or even other activities before coming back. Approach reading the text in a variety of ways: silently, taking turns out loud, assigning portions to groups, and other ways to allow for variety.

Writing: Not all students are comfortable speaking out loud. Writing allows students to express themselves without having to speak in front of others. Encourage students to write not only by answering questions or writing essays but by writing a few thoughts on an index card or keeping a journal.

Video: No doubt about it, we live in a video age. Students are accustomed to being engaged visually. Many excellent videos are available for religious education. However, once again, be sure a video fits your goal. You would not show a video if your goal is to get students to articulate. Likewise, a video should never be a passive event. Ask yourself, "What are my students going to *do* with this video after viewing?" Whether it be a discussion, group work, a poster project, or a written response, students should somehow respond to a video. Make sure it is clear that you are not asking for a review of the video. Instead, you are asking them to express what they have learned, what conclusions they can draw from it, or what questions arise as a result of the video.

Prayer: Prayer *is* a student activity—it is part of the learning curriculum. When we pray with our students, we are teaching them a way of living life that is at the heart of our faith. Prayers should not just be a bookend Our Father or Hail Mary to begin or end class. Prayer should be a group experience, allowing students an opportunity to hear the Word of God and respond through spoken word, silence, song, drawing, and other creative ways of expressing themselves.

Panel Discussion: At times, it is not possible to get your whole class involved in a discussion. As an alternative, you may set up a panel discussion. By selecting several students, you can set up a talk show format in which you engage these students in discussion, inviting them to share opinions or thoughts on an issue while the rest of the class is welcome to react or ask questions. Often, students who are *not* on the panel feel freer to raise their hand because they are not on stage but in the audience.

Lecture: At times, the best way to get information across to students is to lecture. Resist the temptation to make yourself the font of all knowledge...it turns your students into sponges and sponges do not react, they only absorb and even then, only to an extent. Intersperse your lectures with discussion and other activities. When you *do* lecture, make sure your students have a study sheet or a place to take notes so that they are not just passively observing but are involved actively in the learning process.

Games: Involving your students in games can be a lot of fun—it can also be trouble if the games do not have a purpose. Games work well as icebreakers. However, even when breaking the ice, it is helpful if the game has a connection to the lesson so that you can point back to it and use it as a learning experience. Games also work well as a reviewing exercise, enabling you to go over a great deal of information in a lively format. Be sure the attention is on learning and not only on winning. Also, be sure to give clear instructions before beginning and an explanation of the purpose of the game.

Posters: Inviting children to make posters is a positive way of encouraging them to work together and express themselves in non-oral ways. By providing magazines and newspapers, you can invite students to cut out and arrange images that express either contemporary experience or reflect images from Scripture. Likewise, when students present their posters, they are more apt to speak out loud because they are speaking about an object separate from themselves—a good way to get a shy child to speak!

Drawing: Some children do not like to speak in front of others. Others do not like to write. What else can you do? Invite them to draw. I once invited a class of ninth graders to draw a picture of God. The results were fascinating and served as a great way of getting students to talk about their God image. Sure, some children will say they can't draw, but you can ask them to imagine how it feels for those who don't like to speak or write. Another activity related to drawing is to use modeling clay to ask students to express their image of God or the Church or other topics you want to explore.

Music: Judging by the billions of dollars made by the recording industry each year, it is safe to say that music is a big part of our lives. This is true of children as well. Using music in your class is a great way to engage their imagination. You can play music in the background while they are doing some writing or other project. You can use a contemporary song (especially with older children) to introduce a theme or topic and engage them in discussion about the message of the song. Be sure you have some insight into what kind of music the kids are listening to. Bringing in a copy of Simon and Garfunkel's "Feelin' Groovy" just might not be where they are at!

Questions: This tool sounds easy to use, but there is a right and a wrong way to ask questions. Be sure your questions are open-ended and not limited to yes and no answers. Always ask a question, pause, and then repeat it to be sure that children have heard it properly. After asking, pause and wait. Don't panic at the silence. The pressure is on the students to respond. If you've prepared well and asked a proper question, you have done your job—now they have to do theirs. Don't be too quick to call on the same student who always bails you out. By the same token, don't startle children by calling on them before they've had a chance to think about it. You may call on a student who did not raise his or her hand, but be sure he or she will have a good chance of responding. Do not ask questions to stump students. Asking questions is like playing tennis with a friend—you really *do* want them to return the ball.

Guest Speakers: Let's face it, as much as our students may like us, they are always intrigued by the sight of an unfamiliar face coming into the classroom. A guest speaker can have a great deal of impact on a class. Perhaps a Pastoral Associate, a Youth Minister, a Director of Social Ministry, a priest or nun, a missionary, or someone to speak on drug or gang prevention will provide your students with a heightened understanding of your topic. Be sure students are told what to listen for and always integrate the presentation after the speaker has left.

Group Work: Putting children into groups can be very tricky but also very effective when done properly. Group work is an excellent vehicle for teaching cooperation and community. Likewise, group work may be very effective for dividing tasks or breaking down multiple themes to be researched and reported upon. Group work, however, must be very clearly defined. Directions and instructions should be given before placing children in groups and brief time limits should be given so that students know they are under pressure to stay on task. You will need to constantly walk around to make sure that students remain focused and to offer assistance.

Role Plays: On occasion it may be helpful to invite children to act out scenarios from real life experience or from Scripture. Role playing is a way of allowing students to express themselves creatively and will often reveal how they view themselves and others. Like other group work, keep the instructions and time limits clear and concise. Be sure to set guidelines on what type of behavior and language may be depicted. Provide props if they are helpful. Be sure to process after each role play to determine how it contributes to the lesson and avoid the temptation to critique the performances.

Field Trips: Any opportunity to get out of the classroom may provide your students with a refreshing change of scenery. Field trips do not have to be long distance. The most important field trip you can arrange is to the church to show children around and introduce them firsthand to the worship environment. As with any field trip, be sure it is well thought out and organized. Chaperones are necessary to keep little ones safe and older ones under control. Field trips may also double as service experiences if you are able to arrange for children to assist at a soup kitchen or food pantry.

Storytelling: No one is ever too old to listen to a well told story. Little children will be more open to listening to you read a story from Scripture. That doesn't mean that it can't be done with older children. If the story is age-appropriate and does not make the students feel they are being talked down to, it can be very effective. Resources are available for telling Scripture stories in more contemporary language which may catch the ear of your students. Be sure to have questions to follow the story so that comprehension may be tested and the students engaged.

Arts and Crafts: Some children are able to express themselves better artistically. Arts and crafts projects allow children an opportunity to do something fun while at the same time providing you with a vehicle for teaching. Excellent lessons can be taught through arts and craft projects because, as the project is being explained, the story is being told. Be sure you have all of the necessary materials available to make the project progress smoothly.

Troubleshooting

If your color charts are limited, you need to get bigger, better ones. If your selection of student activities is too limited, you need to enlarge it. Do so by slowly acquiring new student activities. You cannot do this all at once. It takes a great deal of time to acquire a large repertoire of student activities. Do it slowly and methodically. At the same time, do not lose sight of the fact that sometimes basic white and off-white are all you need! In catechesis, sometimes the simple activities of reading a text, leading a simple discussion, or lecturing may actually work best for a particular lesson. Finally, if you're not sure about a certain activity, proceed with caution—you would hate to slap a coat of paint on something that would ruin its true beauty. By the same token, you would hate to use a student activity that could actually detract from the learning process.

Catechetical Dos and Don'ts

Do...
- slowly acquire new student activities
- be bold and innovative
- know how to use your activities
- make sure the activity fits your lesson

Don't...
- settle for the same old thing
- select activities just as busy work
- take on more than you can handle
- overuse any one activity

Catechist Quote

"No matter what activities you select for your class, I feel that it is always important to remember that you should teach as if you are talking to every child as an individual. Getting to know their names and using dialogue that addresses each child in your class is crucial for any activity that you select. Calling children by name and engaging them in dialogue during your various activities is a way of letting them know that they are important to you!"

—Sandy Chandler (Intermediate)

A Prayer for Catechists

Lord God, you created this world and all of its array with such beauty and variety. You put the colors of the rainbow in the sky to remind us of your infinite love for us. Help me to participate in your creation by the creative use of variety in my classes. As you filled the skies with stars, the oceans with swimming creatures, the land with plants and animals of all shapes and sizes, help me to fill my classes with a variety of student activities so that the true beauty of your Word will be seen and heard in many colorful ways. Amen.

Chapter Four

Drop Cloths: Preparing for Things that Might Go Wrong

When I paint, I tend to get lazy. I usually figure I can accomplish the job with the least amount of effort. Why bother with masking tape, drop cloths, paint thinner, etc., when I can just get started and be done before you know it? Needless to say, you can guess the outcome. Whenever I attempt to paint without taking the necessary preparations, I tend to knock over a can of paint, drop a brush, or flinch just when I'm painting a tight corner. The result is paint where it shouldn't be: on the glass, on the carpet, and all over me! I've learned my lesson well. Now, whenever I paint, I painstakingly take a good amount of time to tape around all the edges, place drop cloths everywhere, and keep a supply of paint thinner and a wet rag for those unplanned spills. It can be frustrating making all of these preparations when I just want to get down to business and paint. However, in the long run, I have become a much more efficient painter. I've learned that what can go wrong *will* go wrong, so why not be prepared?

Catechetical Drop Cloths

When teaching a class, a million and one things can (and sometimes do) go wrong. As a catechist, you need to become aware of all the things that can typically go wrong so that you can learn to both prevent and recover from common mishaps. Whether it be something minor like a child talking out of turn or a major disruption that brings your class to a grinding halt, you need to be prepared in the same way a painter prepares for the many little things that can ruin a job.

Let's begin by looking at a list of what I call the top ten things that can and will go wrong in the classroom. These are based on my own experience and on discussions with classroom teachers and catechists.

1. Your AV equipment either doesn't show up, doesn't work, or breaks down.

2. You're short on the amount of handouts/materials you were supposed to have for this class.

3. You are emotionally or physically run down and can't find the energy needed to teach this class.

4. Your students totally misunderstood the complex directions you just explained.

5. A smart-mouthed student stumps you with a question you have no idea how to answer.

6. The lesson, video, or text turns out to be a lemon.

7. A discipline problem makes you lose your train of thought and the flow of the class.

8. An interruption (someone at the door) allows the students just the sliver of time they need to go berserk.

9. Someone (a guest speaker or student doing a presentation) doesn't show up.

10. You're finished with your planned lesson and you still have thirty-five minutes of class time to go.

Tips for Cleaning Up Classroom Problems

Some of these problems can be pretty sticky! However, you may be surprised to know that most, if not all, of these can be avoided or at least coped with so they don't ruin your class or you! Let's take a closer look at each.

1. *Your AV equipment either doesn't show up, doesn't work, or breaks down.* The first time I presented this list at a workshop, the prayer leader preceded me with a song featuring taped accompaniment. Just as we waited for the song to come on, nothing happened. Such silence can be deafening! Luckily, we were in a room full of adults. If children were

present, all could have been lost. You don't have to be a technical genius to avoid the problem of AV equipment malfunction. First of all, arrive early to make sure the equipment you need is indeed present. Next, go through a trial run to make sure the video plays, the volume works, the picture comes on, and the tape is the right one. If something doesn't work the way it is supposed to, you'll have time to correct the problem without an audience watching. We've come to rely heavily on AV equipment in the teaching environment. However, the success of AV-reliant lessons still lies in the preparedness of the instructor.

2. *You're short on the amount of handouts/materials you were supposed to have for this class.* As easily avoidable as this problem may seem, it still is one of the most common and annoying teacher problems. Let's face it, we have so many other things to think about and do, we often don't take time to count how many handouts, books, crayon boxes, or Bibles we have on hand for our class. Like a painter measuring the walls to determine how much paint to buy, we need to be very careful to count through all of the supplies and handouts we will use to make sure we have enough. Make sure you have a briefcase or teacher bag in which to organize all your materials. The key to avoiding this problem is simple—organization! A good catechist always takes the time to make sure that the number of handouts is at least equal to the number of students.

3. *You are emotionally or physically run down and can't find the energy needed to teach this class.* You may be very well prepared and excited about the class you are about to teach. Unfortunately at the last minute, you develop a sore throat, your baby spikes a fever of 103, or you and your spouse have an irritating argument about the month's finances right before you leave for class. What's a catechist to do?

Many of these problems are unavoidable—they simply *will* happen. The question is, how will you handle them? First of all, you and your DRE need to have a contingency plan. If you cannot, under any circumstances teach the class, you need to know the proper procedure for arranging a substitute. Likewise, you need to have personal contingency plans in case you need a baby sitter or other personal arrangements made so you can come to class. If you are able to come to class, be aware of the burden you are carrying but do not under any circumstances attempt to take it out on your students or seek solace from them. At times like this, you need to pray for the inspiration you need to acknowledge your burden but then set it aside so that the children can come first. It is not easy, but with the Lord's help, you can overcome your burdens and devote yourself to your lesson and the children.

4. *Your students totally misunderstood the complex directions you just explained.* This is a common problem encountered, especially by new teachers and catechists. Suppose you have a complex lesson involving the use of small groups and a wide variety of materials and tasks to accomplish. You give what you think are good directions and send the students off to accomplish the task. Within a few minutes, no one seems to know what they are supposed to be doing. Frustrating indeed!

To avoid this problem, follow some very simple rules. First, never put students into a group until *after* you've explained the directions for group work. Second, always *repeat* your directions a second time. Third, ask for a student to repeat the directions back to you so you can test their comprehension. Finally, continue to repeat the directions even after the group work or task has begun so that they are continually reinforced. Again, this may seem painstaking, but the alternative is chaos or anarchy—take your pick!

5. *A smart-mouthed student stumps you with a question you have no idea how to answer.* Your class can be going along very smoothly until it happens—the loaded question! You know the type: Did Judas go to hell? or Why can't women be priests? or If we're eating the body and blood of Jesus at communion, doesn't that make us cannibals? Ouch! These questions are not easy to answer in a quick response and during the moment you pause to decide how you're going to answer, panic can set in. Here's what you need to do.

First, if the question is clearly out of line, politely tell the student to hold on to that question until another more appropriate time. Second, if you think the question is reasonable (these questions may often be quite sincere), but you are still stumped, tell the student that they have asked a good question but you honestly don't know the answer at the moment. Promise to get the answer for next class and be sure to begin the next class by taking care of such old business. Finally, if you're working with older students, you may invite someone else to answer the question if they think they know the answer and you think they are capable of doing so. Whatever the case, don't panic. You never signed on to be the fountain of all knowledge. By telling the student you need to research and learn the answer to the question, you model for them what it means to be a disciple of Jesus.

6. *The lesson, video, or text turns out to be a lemon.* Sorry, but if you find yourself in this mess, it means you haven't done your homework! The only way you can find yourself in the middle of a lesson, video, or text passage that is poor material is if you did not preview. Always, always, always be sure to watch a video before you show it to your class; read over the text to make sure it is age-appropriate, interesting, and pertinent; and walk through the lesson in your mind to determine if it will work. Quite often when we have a video to show for class, we tend to relax, thinking that we have less work to do. On the contrary, showing a video means that you will take the time to preview its contents, plan a discussion, and get there early to test the AV equipment. The bottom line is *prepare.*

7. *A discipline problem makes you lose your train of thought and the flow of the class.* We're not talking here about major discipline problems. It's the little problems that can get the best of you. You know the kind: giggling, side talking, a tapping pen, a well-timed burp (or other gastrointestinal sound effects), etc. Your goal as catechist is to stay on course with your lesson. That doesn't, however, mean that you ignore the situation. The challenge is to confront the behavior without stopping the lesson. If a child's attention is wavering, call on

that child to get him or her back into the mix. If a child is making noises that are disruptive while you or someone else is talking, go over and stand by that child and if necessary, place a hand on his or her shoulder to make your presence known. Don't be a stationary catechist—get up and move around the room. Your proximity to students is the strongest deterrent against disruptive behavior. Your moving around allows you to continue the lesson while relying on eye contact, proximity, or a tap on the shoulder to challenge disruptive behavior.

8. *An interruption (someone at the door) allows the students just the sliver of opportunity they need to go berserk.* So maybe berserk is a little extreme, but it doesn't take much for students to get off track. As a catechist, you literally need to grow eyes in the back of your head. In other words, never turn your back on your class. If you are helping an individual student, do so in a way that allows you to continue observing the rest of the class. If someone comes to the door to speak to you, speak to that person while facing your class. This goes against our natural tendency to give someone our full attention when they are speaking to us, but you are committed to devoting your full attention to your class at the moment. Finally, *never* leave your class unattended! Not only do you risk discipline problems, you are also in jeopardy of safety and legal concerns.

9. *Someone (a guest speaker or student doing a presentation) doesn't show up.* You've got it all planned out. The students will do presentations of the posters they've worked on for your next class. The only problem is, three of the five students scheduled to present their poster that day were absent because of the chicken pox going around the parish. Once again, you're left holding the bag. This problem may be unavoidable, but you need to have a contingency plan. Always have plan "B" ready in case plan "A" fails. It need not be elaborate, but you should have some type of activity or lesson ready in case the people you were counting on don't show up.

10. *You're finished with your planned lesson and you still have*

29

thirty-five minutes of class time to go. This is every catechist's nightmare! This happens especially when planning some type of discussion. You picture yourself engaged in a great discussion with students for twenty minutes or so only to find out that they are uttering little more than a grunt here and a groan there and you've completed all your discussion questions in the first five minutes.

The key to coping with this problem is to always *overplan.* Especially as a new catechist, you need to prepare for *more* than you think can be accomplished in your allotted class time. As you become more seasoned, you will develop more of a feel for how long a lesson will take and how much material you need. As you overplan, however, don't bite off more than you can chew. It's just as bad to reach the end of the class period only to find out that you needed five more minutes to bring closure to your prayer experience. The key to over-planning is to be sure you have extra material that is not necessarily crucial to your lesson. If you need to rely on it, fine. If you don't get to it, fine. But don't leave home without it!

Warning!

Don't be alarmed by all the things that can go wrong in your class. This list of things that can and will go wrong was not intended to frighten you. Quite the contrary, if you are well aware of all the things that can go wrong and how to deal with them, you will be able to deal with them much more effectively. Painters don't get frightened by the possibility of spilling paint—they just bring drop cloths.

Words to Remember

Only two words are necessary to understand this chapter on things that can go wrong: *organization* and *preparation.* These words are self-explanatory. If you devote the proper amount of time preparing for your class and organizing your materials, you will either avoid or effectively cope with most anything that can go wrong!

Troubleshooting

Despite being highly prepared and organized, things can still go wrong. The key to anything that comes up in your class is not to panic. If you remain calm and keep your perspective, you will be able to handle any problem that arises.

● ●

Catechetical Dos and Don'ts

Do...
• prepare
• plan ahead
• imagine all the possibilities
• be ready for anything
• remain flexible
• keep the class flowing

Don't...
• get lazy
• panic
• lose focus
• assume
• turn your back

● ●

Catechist Quote

"When you find yourself mopping up the spills of your class day and recalling what seems to have been the worst teaching session of your life, try to recall this lighter moment: A catechist once worked very hard teaching prayers to her wide-eyed second graders. 'Let's pray today for our good friend Cardinal Bernardin, who's been so sick and is in need of the comfort that our prayers will bring.' 'Who?' asked one little boy who had trouble remembering our beloved archbishop's title and name. 'That is a hard name to remember,' agreed the catechist. 'Just try to remember the bird—a cardinal—and then shorten his name to B. I'm sure Jesus will know who you mean when you pray for Cardinal B.' The little boy seemed content with that. At the end of the class, I, in my role as DRE, asked the children who they had prayed for today. This child, in his new found knowledge of prayer and the archbishop's name, excitedly shouted out, 'In our class, we prayed for Robin B!' Talk about needing a drop cloth to scoop that little boy's catechist off the floor!"

—Sharon Allison (DRE)

A Prayer for Catechists

Lord Jesus, things didn't always go as you had planned. When you spoke in your hometown synagogue, they tossed you out. When you tried to meet the minds of the Pharisees, they responded by trying to trick you. When you taught parables to your disciples, they often did not understand. Yet, you continued to find ways to reach people even if it meant making a point by washing your disciples' feet. Help me to be prepared for the unexpected in my classes and to find creative ways to overcome all those little things that can and will go wrong. Amen.

Chapter Five

Primer: Preparing Your Teaching Environment

A popular TV commercial espouses the slogan "Just Do It!" While that advice works for some things, it doesn't work for painting, wallpapering, or teaching a class. First, let's take a look at the examples of painting and wallpapering. These are two ways of bringing out the true beauty of a room. My problem is that I like to start painting and/or wallpapering immediately. However, the right way to do it is to prepare the surface you are going to be working with. Before you apply the paint or the wall-paper, you have to make sure you have scraped, spackled, sanded, cleaned, and most importantly if you're painting, applied a primer. Then and only then are you ready to apply the paint or wallpaper that will truly bring out the beauty of the room and make it last. If you skip all these steps, your results will be seriously flawed or you will fail altogether. How you prepare the surface is the most important step in completing your project.

Paying Attention to Your Surroundings

When teaching a class, the same advice holds true. You need to complete some preliminary steps to prepare the environment you will be working in lest your lesson be seriously flawed or fail altogether. Preparing a classroom for a lesson is not unnecessary fluff or fussiness. It is a way of increasing the effectiveness of your lesson, thus allowing you to tap the true inner beauty of your students.

Jesus paid a great deal of attention to his surroundings when he taught in order to achieve the greatest effect. When he taught the Beatitudes, it is no accident that he gathered his crowd around a mount from which he delivered his talk, creating an image of the "new Moses." Likewise, when Jesus knew the moment of his death was approaching, he took great pains to have preparations made for the room in which the Passover meal would be celebrated so that the environment would be proper for this important celebration. Finally, when Jesus spoke to a crowd of five thousand people, he selected a setting in a deserted spot. When the people became hungry, he made detailed arrangements to have them gathered into groups of fifty or one hundred, "like flower beds," before the miracle of the loaves and fish took place. Jesus used these preparations to heighten the effectiveness of his "lesson," thus emphasizing how he indeed not only satisfied hungers but brought order to chaos and new life (the image of flowers) where there was death (the desert). If we are to teach as Jesus did, we too must take pains to think of our environment and make the necessary preparations to increase the effectiveness of our lessons.

Tips for Preparing Your Classroom

If you were having people over for dinner, you would prepare the environment to heighten the enjoyment and express a mood of celebration and welcome. When we teach, we are hosting a "meal" for our students. We are bringing them nourishment for the spirit and soul. Therefore, we need to take the necessary steps to "set the table."

1. *Pay attention to seating arrangement.* Remember our discussion of how Jesus arranged the five thousand into groups of fifty and one hundred "like flower beds"? Arranging your "crowd" is crucial to your lesson as well. If you teach to students with desks arranged in straight rows facing your desk, what message are you communicating? If at all possible, arrange the desks in a circle or semicircle or some arrangement that encourages interaction and is conducive to prayer as well. Your goal should be to create an arrangement that keeps order but encourages a sense of welcome, comfort, and community while removing intimidation and rigidity.

2. *Make a prayer station your central focus.* What is the central focus of your class? Is it your desk or podium? The chalkboard? In a religious education setting, it is imperative that the central focus of your class be *Jesus.* Once you have created the proper seating arrangement, be sure that the central focus for your children will be images that represent the Word made flesh, namely a Bible, a candle, and/or a bowl of holy water or crucifix. If you truly are encouraging your children to make Jesus the center of their lives, at least make Jesus the center of your classroom.

3. *Hang posters, pictures, and objects.* We live in a very visual age. By the time children reach your classroom, they have been conditioned to receive more visually than orally. Take advantage of this fact by hanging posters and religious images that can reinforce your lesson. Pictures and posters of Scripture stories and the saints can make for an effective addition to your lesson. Small statues and images can add to the message you are teaching as well. Likewise, photos of the children in action can show just how much importance you really place on *them.* If you do not have your own room to put up posters and pictures, you can easily create a portable display panel that you can carry in and out for your lesson and use as a focus.

4. *Use the chalkboard, easel, and overhead projector.* Adding to the visual images of posters, pictures, and objects should be the effective use of your chalkboard, an easel with newsprint, or an overhead projector. One of the most effective things you can do before a class begins is to arrive early and write key phrases, directions, or names, and definitions on the board, easel, or overhead so that when class begins, you can refer to these images without turning your back on your class to write. Likewise, they give the children a definite message that you are prepared and there *is* work to be done.

5. *Organize your supply station.* After Jesus fed the five thousand, he instructed the disciples to gather all of the scraps into twelve baskets. Jesus knew that the key to making the most of resources was to be organized. As a catechist, you will need many resources to conduct your classes, from

handouts and textbooks to pencils, crayons, glue, and scissors. It is important for you to have a supply station to keep all of these well organized and at your fingertips. Whether it be a table, your desk, a shelf, or a cabinet, you need to have your supplies organized so that when you need them for class, you do not have to interrupt your lesson to retrieve them. Again, if you do not have your own classroom where you can store these things, be sure to arrive early to get the supplies you need and arrange them in the classroom so that they will be organized and accessible when needed.

6. *Take advantage of AV equipment.* Jesus didn't have to worry about VCRs or CD players. He did, however, use the medium of his time—the telling of parables. We too must take advantage of the medium of our times. The proper use of AV equipment can enhance a lesson greatly. You do not have to be a technical genius to handle this equipment either. If you are showing a video or playing a tape or CD, be sure you've got it set to the right place and that you know how to turn on the power and adjust the volume. (Don't try this for the first time in front of the students.) It is also helpful to leave the power on so that when it's time to press play, that's all you have to do.

7. *Don't forget name tags.* When you are getting your classroom in order, be sure to remember a name tag for each child. Calling your students by name is a way of honoring them and letting them know that you really are interested in them. It is also a way of keeping order in your class. If a student is misbehaving, it helps to be able to call them by name rather than "Hey, you." In baptism, we were each given a name that is inscribed in heaven. Jesus calls us each by name. We should do no less for our students.

 Warning!
While preparing your classroom is a very important step, don't go overboard! A class that is visually "loud" will detract from your efforts to create the proper atmosphere. Secondly, be aware of financial

restraints, not only on your program and the DRE, but on yourself. You may not have the financial resources to obtain all of the things discussed in this chapter. However, these need not be excessive expenses. With some imagination, most of what you need for your classroom can be found on a very modest budget. Finally, keep in mind that *functionality* is your goal. The classroom is meant to serve you and the students, not the other way around. In the end, while it is true that Jesus gave thought to preparations before he taught, he also was able to teach anywhere at anytime. A catechist friend of mine reminds me that one of her most effective classes was the time she was locked out of her classroom and had to teach in the hallway!

Words to Remember

Prayer Station: A small table in the center of the room with a Bible, candle, and/or bowl of holy water and crucifix placed there as a visual focus.

Functionality: A classroom must be designed to serve the students and the teacher as well as the goals of the lesson. While aesthetics are important, the bottom line is whether or not the design will work for the class activity.

Display Board: Available at office supply stores, a display board or panel is a trifold cardboard/styrofoam poster board that can stand on its own or on a tabletop. It can be used to display posters, pictures, or reports and is especially effective because of its portability.

Overhead Projector: An overhead projector allows you to project images from a transparency onto the board or screen at the front of the room. This is especially effective because it allows you to remain in the midst of the students instead of turning your back to write on a board at the front of class.

Environment: The overall setting within which a people attempt to thrive. A classroom environment refers not only to the room itself, but also to the seating arrangement, the decor, and functionality of all of its contents.

Troubleshooting

If you do not have your own classroom or share it with another catechist or school teacher, you will need to think *portable*. Bring with you whatever you need to prepare your classroom for your lesson. You will need to arrive at your teaching space especially early so that you can make your arrangements.

— If you have stationary desks or are asked to not move the ones in your classroom, your hands are tied to some extent. You may, however, be able to sit on the floor if space allows. Also, speak to your DRE about occasionally moving to an open space like a school hall, chapel, auditorium, or even outdoors. Finally, you may wish to place more emphasis on activities that get students out of their desks.

—If you are in a home teaching environment, you are not off the hook. In fact, you may need to pay attention to these preparations even more so that usual home distractions (TV, music, view of neighbor's kids playing, etc.) don't interfere. Portable display panels and a prayer station can be very effective in a living room setting.

—If you lack the financial resources to prepare your classroom, you need to use your imagination. Several pieces of newsprint taped to the wall can serve as an effective chalkboard. Your own Bible and a small vigil candle can create a nice prayer station. Holy water is free. Have the kids create posters to decorate the classroom if none are available. Name plates can be made from index cards and placed in front of each child instead of adhesive tags. In other words, meager financial resources simply mean that your own creative resources will need to be called upon even more!

—Again, don't panic if you are unable to accomplish some of the things discussed in this chapter. They are meant to enhance the lesson, but if Peter and the Apostles taught the first lessons of Christianity on the street corners of Jerusalem, we too can find ways of teaching our lessons no matter where we find ourselves.

Catechetical Dos and Don'ts

Do...
• be innovative
• be functional
• use creative energy
• use scriptural images
• change as the year goes on

Don't...
• settle for desks in straight rows
• forget to focus on Jesus
• ignore your teaching environment
• use only butterflies and smiley faces
• overdo it

Catechist Quote

"As an arts and crafts teacher, I like to prepare the room with a variety of manipulatives, from cereal (fruit loops for rosaries!) to fabric squares (advent wreaths). I prepare the environment so that the children have an experience that is fun, meaningful, and different. The tone of my classroom, although controlled, is never boring or stuffy. I prepare the classroom to communicate that I am glad to see the children and they know it!"

—Sharon Waicosky (Arts and Crafts)

A Prayer for Catechists

Jesus, before you taught the parable of the net, you made sure you were seated in a boat before the great crowds. You knew how to make the most of your environment for teaching. Help me to make the arrangements I need in my classroom to prepare my students, make my lesson more effective, and bring order and life to my lessons. Help me to arrange my classroom in the same way that you are preparing a banquet for us in your Kingdom. Amen.

Chapter Six

The Spotlight: Shifting the Focus onto Your Students

Why do repairs always need to be done in the darkest, dingiest corner of the attic or basement? It seems that all of the important circuits, pipes, wires, and conduits all end up in a very remote and unlit portion of the house or garage. Getting to them is never easy. Seeing them is even harder. Without my trusty spotlight, I would never be able to change a fuse or reconnect a loose wire in one of those dark corners. Whole areas of the crawl space, attic, or basement that were previously completely in the dark now come to life under the bright beam of the spotlight. Crevices that I didn't even know existed snap into focus under the bright light. And yes, signs of life that I did not know existed become evident under the bright light of the spotlight!

A funny thing happens, however, when I work with a spotlight. Eventually, somehow, the spotlight gets turned and twisted until it is no longer shining on what I need to see but is shining right into my eyes. Needless to say this is uncomfortable, but even more important, it is detrimental to what I'm trying to accomplish. The spotlight is not supposed to be on me but on my repairs.

Illuminating the Entire Class

When I was a student teacher, I was very proud of my first class. I thought I had taught very well. My mouth had a motor on it that never ran out of gas. When class was over, my cooperating teacher congratulated me on surviving, said I did a good job, but bluntly added, "You talk too much!" I thought teachers were supposed to talk! "Yes," he replied, "but not all the time. The spotlight is not supposed to be on you, it's supposed to be on your students. They are the ones who are supposed to perform, not you." This was a Copernican revolution for me, but it made great sense. If I do all of the performing, then I become an entertainer and the students become an audience. The spotlight is in the wrong place.

Some of us enjoy the spotlight more than others. To most, the spotlight is very uncomfortable. Once, when I was doing a catechist workshop, I brought along a very bright flashlight. I asked the catechists to introduce themselves. As they did so, I directed the bright beam right on them like a spotlight. When they were finished, I asked how the light made them feel. Needless to say, most feelings ranged from uncomfortable to annoyed. I explained that in each classroom, there is a spotlight waiting to shine. If we focus it totally on us, we are putting a great deal of pressure on ourselves. The goal of a teacher is to turn that spotlight around and spread it on the entire class. On any one person, it is overwhelming. If it is poured out and diffused over a whole class, it is just the right amount of light to bring about a new focus and a new way of seeing things that otherwise go unseen. As catechists, we need to learn how to shift the focus or pressure off of ourselves and onto the class where it will allow us to see our students in a whole new way.

Tips for Focusing on Students

Catechists tend to put a lot of pressure on themselves to do all of the talking. This is a hard habit to break. Here are some tips on how to shift the focus away from yourself and onto your class.

1. *Look over your lesson plan.* Examine your lesson plan: how much talking are you planning on doing? Sometimes lecture is necessary, but if you are always doing all of the talking, when and how will the children learn to express their faith? Take some of your talking time and brainstorm ways of getting the students involved in bringing forth the material you wish to cover.

2. *Review your goals and objectives.* Remember, your goals

and objectives are not statements about what *you* are going to do, but descriptions of what your students are going to do. If your objectives call for students to articulate an understanding of the Beatitudes, that means that *they* are to articulate it, not you! Look over your goals and objectives and then examine your lesson plan and determine how the *students* are going to demonstrate proficiency in the areas defined.

3. *Identify ways students will demonstrate learning.* Students can demonstrate learning and understanding in a wide variety of ways (see chapter three). Don't rely solely on oral expression. Provide your students with a variety of ways in which they can demonstrate an understanding of material, either through drawing, writing, role playing, poster making, etc. Intersperse these opportunities throughout your lesson. Don't just lecture and then give a quiz. The old image of students as sponges who will soak up the information you offer them is not accurate. If the students *are* sponges, they are saturated with messages they are receiving from a society that bombards them through the media. They will not be able to retain what you offer them. However, studies show that students retain ninety percent of what they *do*. Get your students doing!

4. *Be prepared with open-ended questions.* Too often, catechists will ask questions that result in the answers of yes or no. In frustration, the catechist will give up on discussion and go back to lecture. Be sure to ask questions that are "open-ended," that cannot be answered with a yes or no. For example, instead of asking, "Do you remember your first communion?" you would ask, "What are some of the things you remember about your first communion?" Granted, you may still get one word answers, but if you have more than yes or no, you can at least begin making a list on the board for further discussion.

5. *Develop techniques for deflecting.* Students, especially older ones, know how to put the pressure on catechists by asking difficult questions. Suddenly, you feel the heat of the spotlight right on you! Learn to deflect these questions by shifting the attention off of yourself and onto the question.

Respond to a difficult question by tossing it back at them ("What do *you* think?") or by inviting anyone else in the class to share their thoughts while you compose yourself and collect your own thoughts. Jesus was very good at this. Recall how he often responded to a question with a question. When the Pharisees asked Jesus where he got the authority to forgive sins, Jesus replied by asking, "Where did John get his authority?"

6. **Resist the temptation to talk too much.** I imagine it would have been easier for Jesus if he had given a lecture to his disciples about who he was. Instead, he asked them two questions, "Who do people say I am?" and "Who do *you* say that I am?" The silent pauses between the questions and the answers must have been tense and awkward. However, Jesus, who had become very good at this, resisted temptation. He did not jump in with the "correct answer" but waited for the disciples to offer the best replies they could. As catechists, we too need to resist the temptation to give the answers and instead help our students grapple with the questions of life and faith.

 Warning!

—When we talk about shifting focus and pressure onto the students, we are not talking about using it as a weapon to make a student feel uncomfortable. Don't put the spotlight on any one student for too long. Spread it around. Never use the spotlight as a means to embarrass a student (such as asking a student who has been misbehaving to stand up and recite the precepts of the Church or the Apostles' Creed).

—Don't forget that the spotlight *does* need to shine on you too. Don't use this chapter as an excuse to never speak in class again. Some catechists get lazy and give group work and role plays every class so that they never need to talk. As you plan on how to spread the spotlight around, be sure to give yourself the appropriate amount of time in the limelight. Like a good talk show host, your introductions, timely comments, questions, and conclusions can make the students' input more cohesive and meaningful.

Words to Remember

Focus: This is another word for the "spotlight" or who the attention is on. If you watch a talk show, who is the focus, the host or the guests? It usually shifts back and forth. As a catechist, you need to be sure the focus or attention is not always on you but on the students and the subject matter.

Lecture: This is the teaching method with which many of us are most familiar. It is when the teacher talks and the students listen. Lecture is often necessary, especially when new concepts are being introduced and defined. However, faith is something that is not installed in a person but is brought forth and nourished. Lecture should be only one of many tools used by a teacher to achieve the objectives of a lesson.

Open-ended questions: These are questions that cannot be answered with a yes or no answer, but require some elaboration. For example, instead of, "Did you ever feel sorry for something you did?" an open-ended question would be, "When was a time you felt sorry for something you did?" This puts the focus on the student and requires more thought than a simple yes or no.

Deflection: This sounds like a sports term such as when a goalie deflects a shot aimed at the goal. In much the same way, students will sometimes ask questions aimed at you. They want to put the focus and pressure (the spotlight) on you. A seasoned catechist learns to *deflect* these questions much as a goalie deflects a shot.

The best way to deflect a question is to turn it back on the one who asked it or the rest of the class. This way, you are sharing the spotlight, taking some pressure off of yourself, and allowing yourself some time to gather your thoughts (and your wits!) to respond thoughtfully. Another way of deflecting a question meant to derail your lesson is to respond by saying, "We'll get to that at another time." Finally, if you are stumped by a question, you may also deflect it by calmly admitting that you don't know but you will find out for next class. This is less pressure than attempting to patch together a response that could leave you open to further and tougher questioning.

Troubleshooting

If you feel the pressure mounting while you are teaching, think of the spotlight metaphor. When you feel too much pressure, chances are there is too much focus on you. Don't panic. Gradually shift the focus to the class and away from yourself. Remind yourself that you are not there to perform but to make sure that the students do. By the same token, get used to the spotlight! Stage fright is natural and you will learn to overcome it. Know that if you feel uncomfortable under the spotlight, you can bet the students will. Show by example that it is OK to have the focus on you for a while.

Catechetical Dos and Don'ts

Do...
- move the focus around
- use a variety of teaching techniques
- ask open-ended questions
- think of yourself as a conductor

Don't...
- use the spotlight to embarrass
- talk too much
- be afraid of the spotlight
- rely too much on lecture

Catechist Quote

"In my experience of teaching junior high, I've found it very challenging to get students to open up. They will, however, if you find a topic that they are comfortable with and interested in. I find that role playing is a good way to get them animated. If you take a situation and help them realize that this is very real and they can apply it to their everyday life, then they won't stop talking! Putting the spotlight on students, especially junior-high students, can be very difficult, but once you find a way of making your topic apply to their everyday life, then it's no problem."

—Joe Rudolf (Junior High)

A Prayer for Catechists

Jesus, you once said, "Nothing is concealed that will not be revealed, and nothing hidden that will not become known. What I tell you in darkness, speak in the light." I believe that you have spoken to my students in the dark mysterious corners of their souls and spirits. Help me to shine the light on them so that they will bring out what is concealed and make known what is hidden. Give me the courage and strength I need to resist the temptation to talk all the time. Help me put the focus on my students so that they will come to realize that the real light comes from within. Amen.

Chapter Seven

The Extension Cord: Plugging into the Power of Prayer

I was all set to begin finishing my basement. I had all the paneling and panel nails ready. I had my electric drill out and all the drill bits ready. I put the drill into place to get started, pressed the power button and...nothing. It wasn't plugged in. I looked around and noticed that the nearest outlet was all the way over on the other side of the room. It's frustrating when you have all of the tools ready to complete a project but you're missing the one thing that will get you going: the power or energy to make it all happen!

The Importance of Prayer

Prayer is plugging into the energy and power of God. As a catechist, you may have all of the tools needed to complete your lessons. You may have all of the skills it takes to conduct a thorough classroom activity. Yet, without prayer, it's like trying to drill holes without an extension cord: if you're not plugged in, forget it! Prayer is plugging in to God, both for you and your students. Personally, you need prayer to sustain yourself and your own level of creativity and commitment. Your class needs prayer because without the power of God in our personal lives, all of the doctrine in the world would be meaningless.

Prayer is not just the frosting on the cake of a good lesson. It is not a set of bookends to open and close class. Prayer is the "yeast" that makes the "dough" of our classes come to life. Prayer is the extension cord we need to reach out to our source of energy: our creator God. Prayer is part of the content and doctrine of our lessons. As we pray, so we believe. As we believe, so we pray.

Tips on How to Use Prayer

1. *Pray before you plan a lesson.* Get plugged in right from the start. Before you sit down to plan a lesson or look over the teacher's manual, take some time to ask the Lord to guide you in your ministry.

2. *Make your planning prayerful work.* To remind yourself of the presence of God in your ministry, plan your lessons in a prayerful environment. Light a candle. Put on some instrumental music. Place a Bible on the table next to you. Dim the lights. Do whatever you find helpful to make your work an act of prayer.

3. *Pray before class begins.* Sometime before class begins, say a short prayer asking the Holy Spirit to inspire and guide you. Ask for the help you need to be focused, loving, and creative.

4. *Build prayer moments into your lessons.* Don't just use prayer at the beginning and end of the class. Build some mini-prayer moments into your lesson. If you are teaching about the sacrament of reconciliation, for example, pause for a moment with your class to pray for forgiveness for the times we have sinned. Provide the opportunity for children to offer spontaneous prayer and petitions.

5. *Ritualize.* Include experiences in your prayer celebrations that "ritualize" the topic or experience you are covering. For example, if you are learning about the sacrament of anointing, allow children an opportunity to write down on a piece of paper the name of someone who is sick, fold it up, and place it in a basket next to a candle. Keep it there throughout the lesson.

6. *Make sure prayer is more than talking to God.* All too often, we think of prayer as "talking to God." Prayer is the act of "plugging" into the energy and power of God. This means that the flow of energy comes from God *to* us. God's energy comes to us in a variety of ways. We need to get beyond talk-

ing and listen, use our bodies, and open up to the many symbols and metaphors through which God speaks to us.

Warning!

—Without prayer, we lose our source of energy and power. Without prayer, we lose our enthusiasm and focus. Without prayer, we burn out. Don't ignore the necessity of prayer in your ministry as a catechist.

—Like electricity, the power of prayer is nothing to take lightly. Prayer is powerful. Be prepared for the fact that the power of God may touch one of your students in an unexpected way (e.g. a child begins crying during a prayer experience) and recognize it as part of the prayer experience.

Words to Remember

Ritual: Ritual is a habitual way of doing something. In prayer, rituals include symbolic ways of acknowledging God's power. Blessing ourselves with holy water is a habitual way (ritual) of acknowledging God's saving grace in baptism. Rituals are effective because they go beyond words and rely on symbols and metaphors. The more we use them, the more familiar and meaningful they become.

Meditation: Meditation is thinking about God. When we meditate, we attempt to become aware of God's power and presence in our lives. It is an attempt to get in touch with that which is always there. It is the way we "plug in" to the power of God already present.

Prayer: It is important to define prayer before you attempt to make it a part of your lessons. Prayer is *always* a response to God. God has already acted in our lives. Through prayer, we are acknowledging and responding to God's saving power. Even when we offer petitions, we are doing so in response to the fact that God has touched our lives previously. We are acknowledging that and asking God to do so once again.

Troubleshooting

Prayer is not easy with children. In many cases, you may very well be introducing them to the concept of prayer. Start small. Start simple. Prayers of thanksgiving are often a good place to start because everyone can think of at least one thing for which they are thankful.

—Avoid the temptation of saying that you are too busy to pray, either personally or in class. We are never to busy to grab a bite to eat, even if it's fast food. To skip prayer is to skip the all-important reminder that all we do is in acknowledgment of God.

—Be patient. Children can be uncomfortable with prayer. They can also be immature about it. Don't give up. Employ simple rituals that do not require a great deal of time and concentration. Use them regularly (such as an enthronement of the Bible before each class) so children develop a sense of prayerfulness.

Catechetical Dos and Don'ts

Do...
- make prayer integral and regular
- use more than oral ingredients
- use prayer objects for focus
- involve the children in ritual

Don't...
- skip it because you're too busy
- just do bookend prayers
- do all the talking
- rely only on formal prayers
- ignore formal prayers

Catechist Quote

"In the ten years I have been teaching religious education, I have found that there are many ways of incorporating prayer in my classroom. We have taken a moment where each of us prays silently or taken turns in saying a prayer or leading a prayer we all know. I have even had my students write their own prayers. Sometimes both they and I are surprised at how much more comes out when they write their own prayers. Prayer is a way for the students to stop and think about God and Jesus in their everyday lives. I try to encourage my students to say a prayer at least once a day so that they know that the Mass or religious education is not the only place we think about God: we can pray everyday and take a moment for God."

—Diane Sheeran (Intermediate/Prayer)

A Prayer for Catechists

Lord Jesus, you made prayer a regular part of your life and ministry. Time and again, the Scriptures tell us that you went off alone to pray. You knew that the Creator was your source of power. You knew that prayer was your link to the power of the Creator. Help me to realize the power of prayer in my life and in the lives of my students. Teach us all to pray so that we may acknowledge your power and glory and be energized by your grace. Amen.

Chapter Eight

Sandpaper: Smoothing Out Discipline Problems

The goal of home improvements is to make things look better and work better. It's not always easy getting there, however. We want our finished products to look smooth and neat. Yet, many of the materials we are working with are rough and rugged. After spackling a crack, the surface is rough and needs to be smoothed out. After cutting a piece of wood, the edges are rough and need to be smoothed out. Enter: sandpaper. If it were not for sandpaper, we would run the risk of bumpy surfaces and the danger of splinters. When we use a sander to smooth down a surface, it's like a miracle—smooth sailing.

Rough Edges in Teaching

In teaching, we encounter many rough edges and bumps, namely discipline problems. Left unchecked, these problems can be like a piece of unsanded wood—someone could get a splinter! A good catechist learns how to smooth out, smooth over, and even eliminate discipline problems. Maintaining discipline in the classroom allows the beauty of the children and the power of God's Word to show through just as sanding down a surface brings out the true beauty of a piece of wood. Rather than giving up when faced with discipline problems, learn how to use some tools to smooth them out.

Tips for Maintaining Discipline

1. *Understand the role of discipline.* Good discipline is not an

end in itself. The goal of your class is effective learning. One can have good discipline but still have a poor lesson. The role of good discipline is to remove any obstacles from an effective learning experience.

2. *Identify what the improper behavior is.* One doesn't need to sand down an entire wall before painting, just the rough spots. By the same token, be sure to clearly identify the discipline problems that you need to address. As the old saying goes, choose your battles wisely. Once you have clearly identified the discipline problems that are most troublesome, you can develop a plan for addressing them.

3. *Don't Panic.* When discipline problems arise, the worst thing you can do is panic. Remain calm and in control. Communicating a sense of authority while remaining calm is not only effective, but necessary in developing a long term strategy for combating discipline problems. Losing your cool may work for the moment, but it undermines your credibility in the long run.

4. *Don't interrupt your class.* One of the reasons children misbehave is they know it will interrupt the flow of the class, frustrate you, and bring attention to them. A good catechist learns to deal with discipline problems without stopping the lesson. By using eye contact, placing a hand on a shoulder, or standing next to the "culprit" while you continue to talk, you can minimize the behavior without interrupting the flow of your lesson.

5. *Keep children involved.* When children get bored, they try to create their own stimulation. When you see that a child's attention is wavering, involve the child in the lesson by asking a question or giving a task for him or her to perform. Of course, if you can keep your children busy right from the start, you eliminate a great deal of potential trouble.

6. *Ride your eye, use names, and move around.* If you are completely stationary, you invite students farthest away from you to engage in misbehavior. It is important for a catechist to be on the move. Physically walk around the class as you teach. Keep your eyes moving around as you speak. If you are answering one child's question, move your eyes around

the class so that it is clear you are still speaking to everyone. Most importantly, learn and use your students' names. One of the most effective ways of getting a child's attention is to call his or her name out loud, pause, and direct the question or task to that child.

7. *Check your seating arrangement.* Where children sit can have a great impact on their behavior. How a classroom is arranged can have a great impact on how the whole class behaves. Your seating should be arranged in such a way that no child feels separated or remote from the hub of activity. If a child feels he or she can "hide" from you, the child will take advantage of the situation. Make sure visual lines are open. Likewise, if a child is misbehaving, it could be that he or she is sitting with children that encourage this behavior. Moving a child's seat can effectively reduce bad behavior.

8. *Reinforce good behavior.* Don't just focus on the negative. An effective catechist learns to focus attention on good behavior and reinforce it. When a class is behaving properly, you can reward them with an activity they enjoy doing such as a game or craft project. When a child known for misbehaving shows the proper behavior, be sure to reinforce it with positive affirmation without going overboard.

9. *Make class rules, explain them, and enforce them consistently.* When your class begins, it is a good idea to formulate some rules with the help of the class. Depending upon their age, you should be able to ask them what rules they will need to make the class go well and create a good learning environment. This is especially effective because when you enforce the rules, you can remind them that this is *their* rule. Be sure students know clearly what the rules are and enforce them in a consistent manner so that children know they are to be taken seriously.

Warning!
If you over-sand any surface, you can ruin it. By the same token, too much discipline can backfire. Be sure to follow these rules:

—Never send a child out of the room alone and unsupervised. You are responsible for that child's safety. Children have been known to wander off and even leave the building after being sent out of a room.

—Be careful not to use God as an "enforcer." Some catechists use the good cop/bad cop routine and make God the "bad cop." Understand that when you put God in the role of the enforcer, you are creating a theology of God that is not consistent with our heritage. Children do not need an image of an angry God waiting to dish out punishment.

—Being overly tough on discipline can create bigger problems. For one, you run the risk of alienating your students. They may be so intimidated by you that they will either not respond at all or will simply parrot back to you what they think you want to hear. Secondly, recall that religious education is for most children their most significant experience of church. If it is a negative experience or one that they fear, they will carry that with them for years to come.

Words to Remember

Discipline problems may be catalogued into three distinct categories:

Minor discipline problems: These are the most typical problems that a catechist faces on a regular basis. Examples from this category include wavering attention, distractions, and side talking. While none of these may seem overly serious, they can wear down a catechist. Left unchecked, they can erode the discipline of a class and lead to more serious problems.

Moderate discipline problems: These are problems that can seriously disrupt the flow of your lesson. Examples include children who set themselves apart from the class and refuse to participate, simple mischief such as throwing spitballs or paper airplanes, or talking out of turn. It is more difficult to deal with these problems without interrupting the flow of your class but they can still be dealt with effectively without bringing your lesson to a grinding halt.

Major discipline problems: These are problems that can bring your lesson crashing down around you. Examples include a class activity that dissolves into total chaos due to lack of clear directions, a student sabotaging a lesson by interfering with a piece of equipment such as a VCR, or an incident of dishonesty or disrespect such as stealing or graffiti. In all of these instances, it is important to remain calm and in control and deal with the specific behavior in a manner that will maintain your self-respect and that of your class.

Troubleshooting

In situations that are serious, it is crucial that you consult your DRE, pastor, colleagues, or any other person of authority so that you are not dealing with it alone. On the other hand, you cannot run to these people every time some discipline problem arises. Be sure the situation warrants it. In serious situations, be fair and flexible, and always give children an opportunity to redeem themselves. Negotiating a contract is a way of dealing with the behavior in a concrete and authoritative manner while providing children with an opportunity to work their way out of the bad behavior. Finally, one of the simplest ways of avoiding serious problems is to make sure that no activity begins until everyone is "on the same page." This means being sure that all rules and directions (as well as consequences for violating them) are understood and clarified before you begin any activity that has potential for disruption.

• •

Catechetical Dos and Don'ts

Do...
•make, post, enforce a few rules
•keep your perspective/sense of humor
•be firm and consistent
•show respect for all students

- identify and confront specific behaviors
- pray for guidance
- be positive

Don't...

- turn your back or leave the room
- continually interrupt your lesson
- allow "erosion" to take place
- create a "boot camp" atmosphere
- use sarcasm or criticize publicly
- punish the whole class because of one student
- give up

Catechist Quote

"Maintaining discipline was probably the scariest thing for me as a new catechist and I was never sure I'd be able to handle the older kids. Little by little, though, I found new ways to handle troublesome situations. My best advice for new catechists would be to persevere. As in all things, we learn from our mistakes. I blew some discipline situations early on and I'm sure I'll blow some more. But overall, I've gotten better and my students know what to expect from me and what I expect of them."

—Joanne Grabarczyk (Intermediate)

A Prayer for Catechists

Sometimes I get worried about facing rough situations in my class and dodging spitballs and paper airplanes. Lord Jesus, you faced some pretty tough audiences in your day and even dodged stones! Yet, you stayed focused on preaching the Good News of the Kingdom of Heaven. Grant me the patience, fairness, and perspective I need to face up to the challenges, handle them with calm and authority, and maintain my focus on the lesson I am to teach. In all things, allow me to show love, no matter how frustrated I may become and help me to acquire new skills to handle discipline so that your Word may come to life in my students. Amen.

Chapter Nine

The Toolbox: Increasing Your Supply of Catechetical Tools

I always wanted a bigger toolbox. For years, I owned a hammer, two screwdrivers, and one pair of pliers. I really didn't need a toolbox. Because I had so few tools, I never built anything. I just made a minor repair here and there, certainly nothing creative or innovative. Whenever I needed something done, I called a friend or neighbor, someone who had more tools than I had and could handle the job that seemed insurmountable to me. As time went on, I watched and learned. I also acquired new tools. Little by little, I was able to tackle projects that before seemed out of reach. Finally, I had a reason to get a new toolbox: my inventory of tools was growing as was my ability to handle challenging tasks.

A Teaching Toolbox
The more tools you have in your toolbox, the less intimidated you will be when faced with repairs and improvement projects. By the same token, the more teaching tools you have at your fingertips, the more confident and innovative will you become as a catechist. Most of us begin our work as catechists with a paltry collection of tools, similar to the hammer, two screwdrivers, and pliers I had in my toolbox. We know how to read the text in class, ask some questions, and perhaps lecture a bit. Beyond that, we feel stiff and inadequate. If only we had the tools that the veteran catechist has as he or she glides through class after class with such savvy.

Allow me to share a corny joke with you that illustrates this point. A visitor to a joke factory is being led on a tour around the plant. As he is being led along, he hears the foreman call out over the loudspeaker, "Number seventy-two!" followed by a great big roar of laughter from the workers. After another minute, he hears another announcement: "Number sixteen!" Again, loud guffaws of laughter from the workers. The visitor asks the tour guide, "What are they laughing at?" The tour guide explains, "The jokes are coded by number. When the foreman calls out a number, everyone recognizes the joke and that's why they laugh." The visitor asks, "Can I try it?" Sure, says the tour guide. So the visitor goes up to the microphone and calls out "Number 68!" Nothing. No reaction. No laughter. "What happened?" he asks the tour guide who replies, "Well, I guess some people just tell a joke better than others!"

It's true, some people seem to have the right tools for telling jokes while others do not. When it comes to being a catechist, we sometimes feel the same way. Unfortunately, we often feel like the visitor to the joke factory wondering what tools we lack when it comes to *our* craft. The fact is, some people are better suited to be catechists than others. However, just as most people can learn to tell a joke properly, most people can acquire the skills needed to overcome perceived inadequacy and flourish in the classroom.

Teacher's Tools

Here are just some of the tools employed by effective catechists to improve their skills:

Movement around the classroom. The best teachers get up from behind their desks and move around the class, keeping students on their toes and providing a sense of energy and enthusiasm through their movement. I once knew a teacher who would stand up on top of his desk every so often to emphasize a point! You may not need to be this dramatic, but you should certainly move about in a way that you feel comfortable and that communicates energy and enthusiasm.

Eye contact/riding your eye. Your eyes should follow the same rule as your body, they should move around. One way of engaging students is to engage their eyes as you speak. As you move about the classroom, make sure your eyes are riding around the class as well so that all students know you are aware of them and interested in engaging them in the lesson. This is also a great way of preventing/handling discipline. By literally (almost!) having eyes in the back of your head, you keep students on task.

Voice. God gave you the voice you have. Some people are blessed with golden throats. Others are not. However, you *do* have control over the volume of your voice as well as the inflections needed for emotion and emphasis. Nothing is more boring to a child than a monotonous adult voice. Put some energy into your voice. Use your voice as a tool to make a point or to add authority to your lesson. Vary the sound of your voice to make sure that it is not monotone. If your own voice does not communicate interest in your topic, then you have little chance of getting the students interested.

Facial expression. Children are very in tune with facial expressions. In fact, I believe one of the reasons children stop coming to Mass is because they don't see the joy of the Resurrection in our adult faces! If we are truly preaching and teaching the Good News, then our faces must reflect it. If our faces express the fact that we are tired, bored, irritated, or uninterested, we don't stand a chance with the children. Use facial expression as a way of communicating to your students that you truly have *good* news for them.

Pace. Any runner will tell you that it is important to have a healthy pace for a distance run. Too fast and you run out of steam. Too slow and you lose. The same is true of your classroom activities. An effective lesson contains a varied pace. A good catechist can learn to sense when the pace needs to be picked up or slowed down. Be sure to pay attention to pace as you teach your classes and make adjustments as needed.

Humor. You don't have to become a comedian or an entertainer to be a good catechist. However, children want to have fun. Humor has an important place in faith development. Humor is a way of celebrating. If the gospel of Jesus is indeed good news to be celebrated, then there must be room for humor. A few light moments in your classroom can make children feel at home and comfortable. Appreciate the humor that the children can offer and don't feel shy about adding your own.

Use of visuals. Our children are growing up in a visual age. If you concentrate most of your attention on the text, it can be like trying to swim upstream. Children's visual capacity must be engaged. Use of the chalkboard, an overhead projector, an easel, posters, pictures, objects, etc., can help engage the children more effectively. Of course, videos and computers can be used effectively in class as well but never as a substitute for human interaction.

Tips for Improving Teaching Skills

1. *Videotape or be observed as you teach.* One of the best ways to determine your movement, pace, voice, and facial expression is to videotape yourself while teaching a class. Afterward, sit down with another colleague and assess your style. Another effective way to accomplish this is to ask a respected and trusted colleague to observe you teach a class and offer you feedback on your style and skills.

2. *Establish "comfort zones" in your class.* Sitting behind your desk is a comfort zone. However, if it is important for you to move around the classroom, be sure to look around and determine areas where you are comfortable and visible so that you can move easily from these various spots as you teach without losing concentration.

3. *Record your voice.* If you do not have access to a video tape machine or someone to observe you, at least set up an audio tape recorder to capture the sound of your voice so that you will be able to determine your pace and variety. If your playback confirms that you are Mr. or Ms. Monotonous, practice adding more variety and emotion to your voice.

4. *Pray before a mirror.* This may sound corny, but it works. Often, before I speak to a crowd, I'll pause in front of a mirror to straighten my tie or comb my thinning hair. I use this time as an opportunity to offer a prayer and ask the Lord to help me reflect in my face the grace I feel within. If you have a notion of what your face is portraying before you begin a class, you will be better able to remind yourself to continue

expressing facial enthusiasm for your lesson.

5. *Have a watch or clock visible.* It is important for you to pace yourself as you teach. Catechists can sometimes lose all sense of time. I once observed a catechist take ten minutes on attendance for a children's liturgy of the Word session that would last a total of fifteen minutes. Needless to say, discussion of the Scriptures for that Sunday was shortchanged. Keeping an eye on the time can help you make sure you're not spending too much time on one segment at the expense of others. By the same token, if you are moving too quickly, it is good to glance at the clock to see how much time you have left. Slow down and toss in a few extra ideas to fill in the time.

6. *Lighten up.* Some catechists are so intense that they forget to laugh and smile. My wife occasionally reminds me to smile as I am walking around doing my DRE duties. As administrator, it is important for me to set the tone and help everyone to relax. By the same token, it is important for catechists to be professionally delightful. One can keep order and focus in class and still maintain a sense of humor.

7. *Walk the line between creativity and maintenance.* Most of life involves maintaining a balance and tension between poles. In teaching, catechists need to live within the tension of being innovative and creative and maintaining a sense of order and regularity. Too much of either can be disconcerting to children. Students need to have a sense of order and regularity. By the same token, however, they need to have their creative juices stirred. The effective catechist learns to move between these two poles and achieve a balance and a healthy tension.

 Warning!
New tools can often be difficult to master. By the same token old tools grow dull when ignored or over used. As you acquire new teaching skills, practice them to overcome awkwardness until you have them mastered. Likewise, you need to continually sharpen these tools to keep them at their most effec-

tive level. In this sense, this advice is more important for veteran catechists than for new ones. Veteran catechists are often the ones who will get complacent and forget to move around the class, vary their voice and facial expression, etc. Don't ever take these tools for granted. Sharpen and polish them!

Words to Remember

Feedback: When a microphone is too close to a speaker, it amplifies itself. The result is feedback. As a catechist, feedback is a way of "amplifying" yourself. Feedback is a way of getting a better look at yourself and your teaching skills either through analysis of video/audio tape or observation from a peer.

Presence: Some people have good stage presence, which means that their posture, movement, voice, and facial expression all look very natural. As a catechist, you need to work on your presence so that you too appear comfortable to the children as you teach.

Pace: This refers to the speed with which you are accomplishing a task. If you have a certain amount of time and a certain amount of tasks to accomplish, it is important for you to pace yourself through your lesson. When planning a lesson, you should anticipate the pace you need. As you teach, keep an eye on the time to see if your pace is panning out and make the necessary adjustments.

Monotone: Some people have voices with a natural variety in them. Those that do not are referred to as "monotone," meaning that they speak in only one (mono) tone (sound). A monotone voice can be very difficult to listen to for an extended period. Adding variety, inflections, emotion, and volume to your voice can help increase your effectiveness.

Troubleshooting

—As you attempt to vary your style and approach, don't try to become something or someone that you're not. Variety must go hand in hand with sincerity. Children are very sensitive to what they perceive as "fake." Stay within your comfort zone but gently push the boundaries out so that you become adventuresome.

—Just like the joke factory story, some just "have it," and some don't. God has given you gifts and limitations. Become aware of them. Accentuate the positive. Play to your strengths. Highlight and improve upon the best that you have. Accept your limitations. As hard as we may try, some of us will just never be the next Bishop Sheen or Billy Graham.

• •

Catechetical Dos and Don'ts

Do...
• get feedback
• visualize/emulate a lively teacher
• use your face to express enthusiasm
• ride your eye/make eye contact
• vary the sound of your voice

Don't...
• assume, neglect, or ignore your skills
• try to become someone you're not
• stare at the walls as you teach
• get defensive about feedback
• shout

• •

Catechist Quote

"'It's just not as much fun as when *you* were here!' This is the comment my former fifth grade student made to me after my teaching assignment was cut short by the premature birth and subsequent four-month hospitalization of my son. Obviously flattered by her comments, I pursued the conversation to see just what it was that I supposedly did right! It turns out that 'fun' for this fifth grader boiled down to her impression that I was sensitive to fifth graders' needs for welcome, fellowship, activity, and even food! These were the tools that helped me to make discussions, activities, and participation meaningful to their lives. As we catechists establish meaningful relationships with our students and attempt to put ourselves in their shoes, we will be better directed in our tasks as effective catechists, utilizing all of our tools to affirm them as people!"

—Gail Kuebel (Intermediate)

A Prayer for Catechists

You must have had the right "tools," Lord, because when you spoke, the crowds were "spellbound" and "amazed" because you "spoke with authority." Your good news is still spellbinding and amazing and your Word carries authority. Help me as an instrument of your grace to use the tools you've given me to bring out the power of your Word. Never let me stand in the way of your Word or dull its power through my own complacency. Rather, sharpen and polish my tools that I may allow the energy and enthusiasm of your good news to leave my students spellbound and amazed by your teaching. Amen.

Chapter Ten

The Broom and Dustpan: Cleaning Up Your Classroom

I tend to make quite a mess when I'm repairing or redecorating. If I'm sanding wood, I get dust all over the place. If I'm cutting with a power drill, I get wood shavings all over. If I'm wallpapering, I get scraps of wallpaper all over the floor. If I'm assembling something, I end up with nuts and bolts strewn all around me. Heaven help me if I have to find something in the middle of all this mess!

Over the years, I've learned to keep a broom and dustpan nearby so that every once in a while I can clean up the mess and see where I've left my tools and how much progress I'm making. It's amazing sometimes when I clean up a little bit and realize how nice everything is beginning to look. It encourages me to continue on and complete the project.

Maintaining a Sense of Neatness

Teaching children is not always a neat process. Especially when we are trying to be creative catechists, we find that our classes can develop a chaotic appearance at times. It is important for our own sanity and for the benefit of the children that we maintain a sense of neatness when we gather. For ourselves, we need to be able to have a clear sense of *tangible* progress.

When you work as a catechist, as well as in any other pastoral ministry, you are dealing in a very *intangible* field. It is not easy to determine progress. How does one know when one has touched a person's life or shaped their faith? This is very difficult. For that reason, it is important to build in tangible signs of progress. If you are able to see visible evidence of learning and progress, you will feel more effective as a catechist. Likewise, the children need to see that they are accomplishing something. We are all aware of how children will respond with, "Nothing," when asked what they learned in school or religion class today. If we can provide them with tangible examples of what they've accomplished, they too will see progress in their learning and growing.

Tips for Cleaning Up Your Classroom

1. *Before class.* Before you begin repairs or redecorating, you need to be sure the room is clean and in order because before long, you will make enough mess of your own. Likewise, a job seems twice as overwhelming if it is surrounded by a mess. The same is true of teaching a class. It is imperative that you and the students are entering a learning space that is clean and neat. It is as if you are having people over for dinner. You need to be sure that everything is clean lest your guests assume that the food too will be less than the best quality. As a catechist, you want them to know that the food you will be serving is of the highest quality. If children see a mess upon entering a room, they will be more than happy to add to it. Likewise, a messy classroom is conducive to messy behavior, i.e. poor discipline. Be sure to arrive early to clean up whatever mess was left from the previous group that used the room.

2. *During class.* As class is progressing, it is important to give specific instructions for keeping things neat and organized. If your students need to move around, use materials, distribute papers and texts, etc., then you know that the possibility of a mess is very real. Clear instructions are key to maintaining a sense of order. Likewise, as a classroom experience is progressing, it can be very effective to take a brief time-out to straighten things up in anticipation of finishing. By doing so, the children will also begin to see the progress in your lesson that has a clear beginning, middle, and ending.

   Finally, a good rule of thumb is to line up. Lining up materials *and* children is a very effective way of keeping order. Imagine you are assembling a new bike. You need to line up all the nuts and bolts and screws lest you encounter total chaos. Lining up text books, scissors, paper, glue, handouts, etc., is a way of keeping order as the lesson progresses. Likewise, lining students up is a very important way of maintaining discipline and order in your classroom and allowing progress to be achieved. Whenever students have to move from one place to another or come forward to receive materials, it is crucial to line them up so that you can see how much progress you're making with each child.

3. *After class.* As class is coming to an end, it is important to have the students straighten out the room so they can see that order is a must. Children should be responsible for gathering up materials and textbooks, straightening out tables, chairs, and desks, and displaying their work on bulletin boards or posters. In this way, they are able to see the progress they and the class are making. Like a decorator standing back to see how nice the wallpapering is coming along, you and your students also need to stand back and see just how beautifully you have participated in God's creation as a result of your class.

 Warning!

A messy classroom is an invitation for messy behavior. Children walking into a class that communicates chaos, carelessness, or confusion, will respond with behavior befitting the environment. Discipline problems and inattention are exacerbated by a messy classroom.

—Don't *over*do your attempts at neatness. Everyone loves a home that is clean but lived-in. By the same token, children need to feel comfortable in their learning space. Neatness is important, but not at the expense of comfort.

—Don't allow "housekeeping" issues to overtake learning. I've seen some catechists spend so much time and emphasis on neatness issues that the lesson itself takes a backseat and is lost. Keep your perspective so that the children will be able to keep theirs.

Words to Remember

What do we mean by *tangible* and *intangible?* Simply put, something that is *tangible* can be touched, felt, seen, and measured. It is "concrete." A tabletop is tangible. A stop sign is tangible. A hug is tangible. When something is *intangible* it cannot be touched, seen, felt, or measured. Love is intangible. Faith is intangible. Spirit is intangible. As catechists, your work is often intangible. You have no way of knowing whether you are shaping children's faith or building their relationship with God. What we need is *evidence.* A hug is tangible evidence of the intangible reality of love. In our classes, we need to develop tangible evidence of the growing presence of God's intangible grace. By maintaining a sense of neatness and order in our classes, we are better able to focus our attention on such tangible evidence of progress in our faith lives.

Troubleshooting

Because you work in such an intangible field as catechesis, it is important that you include tangible signs of progress both in and out of your classes. One of the reasons I like to do repairs and decorating at home is because it gives me a solid sense of accomplishment. If I only worked in catechesis, I might never feel this sense of achievement. For my own sanity, I need to have healthy diversions that give me a sense of accomplishment in a tangible way so that when I go back into the realm of the intangible, I will be better able to handle it. By the same token, I need to remind myself that the children too need tangible evidence of their learning. For this reason, I have always insisted that arts and crafts and music be a part of my religious education curriculum. In both of these endeavors, children feel they are accomplishing something tangible, whether it be creating a rosary out of Fruit Loops or learning to play a song on handchimes.

● ●

Catechetical Dos and Don'ts

Do...
•prepare your room before class

_____ **69** _____

- keep your materials organized
- take a time-out to straighten up
- have children straighten up before leaving
- display children's work/accomplishments

Don't...
- ignore neatness/organization issues
- overdo your attempts at neatness
- let housework overtake learning
- make children uptight
- be afraid of reasonable mess

Catechist Quote

"First thing on my agenda, I arrive early for my class so I can write prayers on the board that we will use in the lesson. I take a little time to pray and ask the Holy Spirit to enlighten me and my children. I always have their books, pencils, and materials ready and in place. My room is always neat! I make sure of that when I come in the classroom and when I leave. During class, I like to have children act out biblical stories so they can really see the lesson before their eyes. At the end of class, we tidy up the desks and leave quietly. I give the children the kind of care that allows them to unfold their God-given abilities as gently and beautifully as a rose unfolds its petals for all to behold!"

—Rosemary Watts (First Communion)

A Prayer for Catechists

Jesus, when you fed the five thousand, you sent your disciples to clean up and collect the scraps that were left over and filled twelve baskets! You knew that people needed to see the full power of the sign you were providing for them. Help me to use the same wisdom in organizing my classes and gathering up all the "scraps" that are left over so that the children may see the miracle that is taking place within their midst. As their knowledge of your Word multiplies like so many loaves and fish, may they come to recognize the true tangible Bread of Life that is feeding them each time we gather. Amen.

Chapter Eleven

Instruction Manuals: Using Textbooks and Teacher's Manuals

I'm not one for working with electricity. Wires scare me and for a good reason: they're dangerous! So, needless to say, when I have to fix an electrical problem around the house, I get pretty nervous—and so does my wife! She's convinced that I will either fry myself or blow up the house. I fear I may accomplish both. You can imagine, then, that when I have to complete some electrical work around the house, my handy home improvement manual is nearby and my wife is far away. Recently, I needed to replace some light switches that had some loose connections. Right there in the middle of all my pliers and screwdrivers was, of course, my home improvement manual open to the chapter on electrical repairs. I read a little, then worked a little, read a little, and worked a little. Lucky for me, I completed the repairs, my house is still standing, and my wife hasn't given up on me!

Using Catechetical Texts and Manuals

A textbook is a tool, just one of many tools. Unfortunately, in many classrooms around the world, the textbook is ninety percent of the total content of the lesson. Catechists and teachers everywhere need to learn that the text is a means toward an end, not an end in and of itself. All too often, the scope of our lessons is based on what chapter we will cover rather than what our goals and learning outcomes (objectives) are. Think back to my electrical repair story. I could memorize the chapter on electrical repairs, but unless I close the book and get to work applying the theory and suggested procedures, my light switch will remain broken. The same is true in our classes. The goal of the lesson is not to complete the text but to provide our children with an experience of Jesus.

Tips for Using Texts with Your Class

Luckily for us, many excellent catechetical texts and manuals are available for our religious education programs. While it is true that texts are not the sole source of our lessons, they do play an enormous role in our overall classroom experiences. While keeping the proper perspective on the role of texts, let's take a look at some tips for using texts and teacher's manuals more effectively:

1. *Be aware of your students' level of aptitude.* Before reading or working with a text, be sure it is appropriate for the age level and aptitude of your students. Your DRE will no doubt play an important role in this assessment, but you are the one in the trenches. Be sure that your text is a tool that will assist, not frustrate your students.

2. *Preview the material you plan to cover.* Some of the texts at our fingertips are so good that they can lull us into a false sense of complacency. It is quite easy for a catechist to assume that the upcoming chapter or section of text will be a breeze. Beware! It is crucial to preview the material you plan to cover to be sure it is on target with your goals and objectives and contains no material that you find overly challenging for your students or yourself.

3. *Give your students an overview of what they are about to read.* A mistake that is commonly made by catechists is the habit of beginning class with a prayer followed by the instructions, "Open your book to page thirty-five and Andy begin reading." First of all, the students have no notion of what your goal for the class is other than to read the text. Secondly, the students have no concept of *why* they are reading this text and to *what* they are supposed to pay attention. Reading or working on a section of a text requires an introduction and brief overview of what you are about to read or do so that students are predisposed to pay attention.

4. *Employ a jigsaw format.* If you need to cover a substantial

section of a text, it can be overwhelmingly boring to simply read it through as a class. A jigsaw is a format that breaks the text and the class into smaller parts. Sections of the text are assigned to various groups. Each group reads their section and then reports back to the larger group, summarizing the main points of their assigned piece of the puzzle. When each group is finished, it is as if a giant jigsaw puzzle has been put together by your class.

5. *Identify vocabulary words and key phrases.* If your annotated text or teacher's manual has not already done so, you need to identify words that should become part of your students' vocabulary as well as key phrases or ideas that should be highlighted. Previewing your text ahead of time allows you to identify these words and phrases and place them on the board for quick reference.

6. *Be aware of the pace.* Reading a text can grind your class to a halt. While it may be necessary to cover sections of the text in your lesson, be aware of the pace of your class. Break up the reading of text sections so that they are interspersed with activities and discussion that will keep your students alert.

7. *Carefully look over the teacher notes in the margin.* Most catechetical texts come with either an annotated text or teacher's manual that provides liner notes or a whole section in the margins of each page providing background on the text and suggestions for discussing and implementing the ideas covered. These teacher notes can provide you with some excellent ideas for making the text come alive and connecting it with your students' lives.

8. *Develop additional questions and activities.* Use the text and manual as a springboard for adding your own discussion questions and classroom activities.

Warning!
Don't use the text as the only source of content for your class. Faith is not contained in a book. If it were, we could simply have our students memorize their

texts and the Kingdom would be fulfilled! Faith is a way of life. A text is one tool that acts as a road map along the way.

—Maintain a critical eye. Even within excellent texts and manuals, you may find sections that are just not up to snuff. If you are not taking sufficient time to prepare and preview your text, you may find yourself covering a section of text that is just plain bad.

—Texts can be biased: racially, theologically, ideologically, etc. Be aware of the biases prevalent in your text. A text written with anglo, upper middle class, suburban youth in mind may be insensitive to the experience of inner city youth of various ethnic backgrounds and economic status. Similarly, some texts are written with almost fundamentalist-like ideology. Be sure you are aware of the biases that exist in your text and be prepared to deal with them.

—Don't equate completing the text with achieving your goal for the lesson. Some of your best lessons will be those during which you don't even touch the text! Be open to the Spirit.

Words to Remember

Content: Like a bottle holding its contents of water, sugar, food coloring, and preservatives, every lesson has its content as well. The content of your lesson is *all* of the ingredients or tools that are being utilized to achieve the goals and objectives of your classroom experience. The text is only one tool and should not be equated with the content.

Teacher's manuals: If you do not have one, get one! Most children's catechetical texts are accompanied by a teacher's manual that provides the catechist with a step-by-step outline for the whole lesson, including ideas for relating the lesson to the children's life experience.

Annotated text: Some programs do not have a full teacher's manual but instead supply an annotated text or a copy of the children's text with key words and ideas highlighted or underlined and suggested questions for discussion included in the margins.

Troubleshooting

—You may be into a lesson before you realize that a text may be outdated, dull, ineffective, or biased. If this occurs, be prepared to move away from the text and into an activity or discussion that will be more in line with the goals you have set for the class. Always have plan "B" ready!

—While focusing on reading from the text, you will discover that some children cannot read well. Never allow a child to be embarrassed by forcing them to read a text of which they are incapable. If a child is stumbling through a section out loud, gently help them through and then ask for someone to assist them by taking over. Take note of the child's reading difficulties and encourage the parents to work with him or her or ask another student to act as a tutor.

• •

Catechetical Dos and Don'ts

Do...
•preview the text
•use texts as a resource
•break up the reading of the text
•take care of texts (they're expensive!)

Don't...
•stay with a poor text
•equate completing the text with achieving goals
•use the text as the only source of content
•use texts beyond your students' aptitude

• •

Catechist Quote

"Thank heavens for the teacher's manual! Reading through each lesson prior to walking into the classroom helps me to feel more confident, relaxed, and convinced that I can get through the lesson. I feel that I have a better handle on seeing the lesson through the kids' eyes instead of only through my own. The teacher's edition gives me insights as to how the children might comprehend and/or question the text. My advice on teacher's manuals: don't leave home without them!"

—Jan DeBoer (Primary)

A Prayer for Catechists

Lord, when you entered the synagogue in Galilee, you were handed the text and read from the prophet Isaiah. But you didn't stop there. You added a new insight or "twist" to the centuries-old text and stirred up a great deal of controversy! Help me to go beyond the texts that are handed to me and stir up something of interest to my students so that they too may be challenged. Help me to use the texts assigned to me as a catalyst or stepping-stone to the fullness of your Word—a Word that does not simply fill space on a page but has the capacity to change lives forever. Amen.

Chapter Twelve

Photographs, Illustrations, and Diagrams: Looking to the Bible

I never buy a cookbook that doesn't contain photographs. Before I go into the kitchen and try cooking something, I want to *see* what it is supposed to look like when it's done. The same is true whenever I am attempting to build or repair something. I need my home improvement manuals to offer photographs, illustrations, or diagrams of the project at hand so I can get a clearer sense of what the finished product is supposed to look like. After I've had an opportunity to visualize it, I am better able to go back and begin applying the step-by-step directions, having in my mind a picture of what I am striving to complete.

The Bible as an Illustration

When we teach religious education, we are attempting to equip our children with the knowledge and skills necessary to live a Christian life. What is that supposed to look like? It would help if we had some illustrations, photographs, or diagrams that could show our children an image of what the life of a Christian is supposed to look like.

The fact is, we *do* have a book of illustrations that gives us numerous images of how to respond to God's call and live a life of faith. The Bible is not only a book, it is a *collection* of books (seventy-three in all) that illustrates for us the stories of the people of Israel and the early Christian community, as both struggled to live lives of faith and determine the will of God.

Unfortunately, many people approach the Bible as a "how-to" book, or a manual of blueprints that provides accurate step-by-step instructions for living every possible human situation. The Bible is not that specific. Instead, the Bible tells us stories of people who attempted (with mixed results) to live out what they believed to be God's will for them. We are meant to use these stories as illustrations so that we can learn how our lives are supposed to look.

When I build or repair something, it never quite comes out looking exactly like the diagram in the home improvement manual. Likewise, when I cook, my dishes never turn out looking exactly like the photographs in the cookbook. I need to make changes and adaptations based on my own circumstances. Yet, the photos and illustrations acted as a guide. The Bible is to be used in much the same way. Our lives are not the same as the lives of those in the Bible stories. Yet, their stories can act as illustrative guides for us so that we can make the adaptations we need to respond in faith to our God in the present day.

Tips on Using the Bible

1. *Familiarize yourself with the Bible.* If you wish to introduce students to the Bible, make sure that *you* have become friends with the Bible first. If all you have at home is that huge hardbound King James version that has served as a family heirloom for decades while collecting dust and going unread, then you need to acquire a smaller soft-cover *New American Bible* (the translation used in the lectionary) that you can begin reading and praying with on your own. Ask your DRE or pastor to assist you in acquiring one.

2. *Read and pray the Bible.* The best way to get to know the Bible is to begin reading and praying with it on your own. Don't read it from beginning to end as you would other books. The Bible is a *collection* of books (I call it "God's library"). Begin with a book that you are attracted to (Psalms, the Gospel of Mark, and Acts of the Apostles are good places to begin) and read a brief passage each day or several days per week. Reflect on the passage, asking yourself what the

Lord is saying to you. Pray to the Lord, asking for wisdom and guidance in understanding God's will. As you do this, you will gradually become more familiar with the Bible.

3. *Enthrone the Bible in your class.* You want to be sure that children recognize the Bible as something sacred. Place it in a prominent place in your room, either in the center, directly in the front, or in a special corner of the room. To enthrone the Bible means to give it a look of prominence. Putting it on a stand with a candle and cross nearby creates a sacred space for which the children will develop reverence. Use cloths and fabrics that reflect the liturgical seasons so that children see the Bible as connected to the celebration of the Eucharist.

4. *Use the Bible regularly in class.* Begin using the Bible on a regular basis in your classes. I found that it was often helpful to select a passage that was intimately connected to the topic of that lesson, and use it as part of the prayer experience for that lesson. Don't limit the Bible to prayer, however. Feel free to bring in a biblical story at any time during your lesson to illustrate a point.

5. *Bring the Bible stories to life.* Be sure to select stories and passages that can be either proclaimed creatively, dramatized, role played, drawn, or viewed on video. It is important that children see these stories come off the pages and come to life so that they can begin making connections to their own life experiences and circumstances. If Bible stories are indeed meant to be used as illustrations, it is helpful to be able to *see* them, not just listen to them.

6. *Stay in touch with the lectionary.* If you are having trouble figuring out where to go to select Bible stories, use the guide that is provided for the whole church: the lectionary. Get hold of a Sunday missal that provides you with the readings for each Sunday Mass. It is very valuable to take time to prepare your children for the readings they will hear in church the following Sunday. Likewise, these readings keep you in tune with the liturgical cycle of seasons so that the children will not only become more familiar with the Bible but with the liturgical seasons as well.

7. *Use Bible stories after you've touched on students' life expe-*

rience. Unlike illustrations in a cookbook or home improvement manual that we look at before we begin, Bible stories are illustrations that are best used *after* we've had a chance to tap into children's life experiences. Children are then better able to connect their story with the story being told in the Bible. This validates their experience and places it within the context of the broader experience of the church and salvation history.

Warning!

—The Bible is quite complex. Perhaps your awareness of this has kept you from jumping into it. The important thing to know is that while the Bible is complex, it is also simple. It is basically telling stories of how people throughout the ages have attempted to hear God's call and remain faithful to it and what happened when they succeeded or failed. On the one hand, don't avoid the Bible because it is so complex. (I call this *bibliophobia* or fear of the Bible!) On the other hand, don't jump into the Bible without the proper preparation and background. Materials providing a better understanding of the Bible can be obtained from your DRE, library, and bookstore.

—Don't get hung up in literal interpretations of the Bible. In any story you are using, help your students to search for the meaning or *truth* to the story that they can apply to their lives. Bible authors very often glossed over facts because they were more concerned with relating the truths of their experience of God.

For this reason, it is important to distinguish between truth and fact. Something can be true but not be a fact. For example, if I say, "It is raining cats and dogs," you know it is not a fact that canines and felines are falling from the sky. However, my statement conveys truth: it is raining very hard. Bible stories must often be understood by using the same approach. Make every attempt to get beyond the facts to discover the truth of the story.

Words to Remember

Fundamentalism: Some Christians believe that since the Bible is the inspired Word of God, every passage must be interpreted literally. Fundamentalism views the Bible as the unerring Word of God and does not distinguish between truth and fact as discussed above. A fundamentalist would say that if the Bible tells us Jonah was swallowed by a whale, then it literally happened. This approach to interpreting the Bible is fraught with problems that limit the reader's ability to apply the truths to contemporary experience.

Contextualism: The Catholic approach to interpreting the Bible is not a fundamentalist one. In other words, it does not interpret the Bible literally word for word. Rather, a contextualist approach attempts to look at the whole passage in context and determine what meaning or truth is being conveyed to the reader beyond the facts of the story. Thus, a contextualist would not be as concerned with the issue of whether Jonah was indeed swallowed by a whale but the truth being conveyed: the futile attempt of running from God's will can be likened to being swallowed up in the darkness.

Testament: As you know, the Bible is divided up into two parts: the Old or Hebrew Testament and the New or Christian Testament. The word *testament* means *covenant* or *agreement*. The Hebrew testament is the pact made between God and Moses on Mount Sinai: Israel shall follow God's Law of love and God will be Israel's God steadfastly. The Christian Testament is the covenant sealed by the blood of Christ: Jesus died for our sins and rose from the dead so that we may have eternal life and lay down our lives for others according to his example.

Gospel: Most of the stories you will use in class will come from one of the four gospels (Matthew, Mark, Luke, and John). It is important, therefore, that you and your students know that the word *gospel* means *good news*. The good news is that we have eternal life in Jesus through the forgiveness of sin. As we use gospel stories in our classes, it is important that we proclaim them in such as way that children will know that the news is good.

Troubleshooting

—Trying to find something in the Bible but can't? Don't give up. Here are several tips. First, get a hold of a biblical concordance or see if your DRE has one or can acquire one. A biblical concordance is a reference book that assists you in locating passages, people, themes, and events in the Bible. It also provides background on topics to help you understand them better.

—It is important to become familiar with the table of contents of your Bible. Learn the abbreviations to books of the Bible or at least know what page of the table of contents lists these abbreviations. Your familiarity with the table of contents of the Bible will save you a great deal of time attempting to locate passages. Think of the table as a card catalogue to God's library.

—Become familiar with the proper notation used for biblical passages: book, chapter, and verse. Many catechists are intimidated by a notation such as 1 Kgs 3:1-7,9. Using your table of contents, you will find the abbreviation to stand for the First Book of Kings, chapter three, verses one through seven, and verse nine. The table of contents will then help you locate the page number.

• •

Catechetical Dos and Don'ts

Do...
•read and pray the Bible on your own
•use the Bible regularly in your classes
•ask what the meaning of the passage is
•have children dramatize Scripture stories

Don't...
•limit yourself to the gospels only
•try to read the Bible cover to cover
•interpret the Bible literally
•avoid the Bible like a plague

• •

Catechist Quote

"As a catechist leading Scripture study for adults, I have found that reading and discussing the Scriptures with others has opened up for me a whole new way of knowing God! Through the stories in the Bible, the people in the stories, and the outcomes, my heart has become more open to God, allowing God to show me the way and strengthen my faith. Listening to others' interpretation of the Bible has often been like a light bulb going on for me. It makes God's good intentions and love for us so much easier to see. Likewise, reflecting on the lectionary readings makes the homily easier to understand and enjoy. Reading the Bible privately has become very satisfying and comforting for me. It brings a feeling of serenity after a long day...something every catechist needs!"

—Dianne Robertson (Adult Scripture Study)

A Prayer for Catechists

St. Paul tells us that "from your infancy, you have known the sacred Scriptures, the source of the wisdom which through faith in Christ Jesus leads to salvation. All Scripture is inspired of God and is useful for teaching" (2 Tm 3:16). Help me, Lord, to better know you through the stories of Scripture so that I may be filled with your wisdom. Guide me in using the stories and "illustrations" of Scripture in my classes so that children will learn the way that leads to salvation. Amen.

Chapter Thirteen

Iced Tea: Knowing When and How to Take a Break

Several years ago, the Midwest suffered through a terrible heat wave with temperatures soaring into the nineties and hundreds. Of course, that was the summer I decided to paint my garage! With the heat index up around 110 degrees, I knew I was going to be in for some pretty tough work. I enlisted the help of a couple of teens and the three of us got to work scraping away the old paint. In the heat and humidity, we could only last about fifteen minutes at a time before we needed to take a break, come into the air conditioned living room, and sip on some iced tea. Not only was this something we wanted to do, we absolutely needed a break for our own health and safety. As the work progressed, we built in times for taking breaks and getting refreshment to avoid heat exhaustion and dehydration. The result was that we survived and my garage finally got the new coat of paint it was thirsting for.

Taking Time Out in Class

I can't emphasize enough the importance of this tool for catechists. In our fast-paced world, taking a break is frowned upon. It is seen as inefficient. Maybe even lazy. In our classes, we are often wondering how we are going to accomplish all of our lesson given the small amount of time we have. How on earth are we supposed to build in time for taking a break?

The fact is, building in some break time for your classes is a tool that can and will increase the effectiveness of your lessons.

Just as I needed to refuel and reenergize myself as I worked on my garage that hot summer, we need to refuel and reenergize both ourselves and our students so that we can come back to our lessons with renewed vigor and enthusiasm. Without some type of break or time out or change of pace, both catechist and students will dry out, lose energy, and decrease in efficiency. When this happens, our work gets sloppy and perfunctory. We just want to get it over with. By learning to take the right kind of breaks at the right time, you can actually increase the effectiveness of your lessons.

Tips on Effectively Using Breaks

We live in a video age. Children watch endless hours of TV each day. The types of TV programs that children tend to watch generally last thirty minutes. During that thirty minutes, there are usually three commercial breaks, meaning that the attention span of most children is conditioned to last between ten and twelve minutes. When we get them for religious education classes, we expect that they will give us their undivided attention for forty-five minutes to an hour. It is no wonder that after a few minutes, we find ourselves encountering our first discipline problem! Here are some tips for working breaks into your classes.

1. *Have breaks built into your lesson.* TV commercials do not occur by accident; they are planned. By the same token, we should plan ahead to have some kind of break or change of pace in our lesson. If your lesson plan calls for you to read from the text for forty-five minutes, realize that you are going to be in trouble. Plan ahead to break up that block of reading with some kind of variety or change of pace.

2. *Breaks must be organized.* Taking a break from your lesson is not a small period of anarchy built into your lesson plan. Any break that you build in must be planned out and organized. Rules and directions must be clearly announced and understood. No break should lead to chaos. Put limits and parameters on what is allowed and stick to them.

3. *The best breaks are educational.* The best TV commercials are those that are either entertaining, informative, or both. By the same token, the best breaks we can plan for our classes

are those that are entertaining and informative, in short, educational. Rather than just telling students to stand up and stretch or get a drink of water, utilize a break to play a short game that will illustrate a point that can be used when you return to the lesson. Likewise, you could use a break to help students get to know one another, especially if the lesson calls for them to be working together in a few moments. Many books are available that provide hundreds of ideas for icebreakers, crowd pleasers, and group games.

4. *Keep your fingers on the pulse of your class.* It is important for catechists to be aware of and sensitive to the mood of their students. You will be the best judge of when to take some kind of a break and what kind of break is needed to increase the effectiveness of your lesson. If students are lethargic, perhaps you need to call a break, open the windows, let in some cold air, and do a few calisthenics. If your class is overly antsy, perhaps you need to call a quiet time to let students calm down and get in the right mood for the lesson.

5. *Include prayer as part of taking breaks.* Prayer can be an effective way to take a break. A friend of mine once told me that near the end of a long lesson, she and the students seemed to be running out of gas. She told her students that she was going to go over and sit quietly on the carpet in front of the prayer station for the last few minutes of class and that anyone could join her if they wished. To her surprise, a good number of students came over and spent the last few minutes of class in quiet prayer together! In our noisy society, this quiet moment was appreciated by all. Prayer can be an energizing and refreshing break from your lesson while still remaining a part of your lesson.

 Warning!
—If you ignore the need for taking breaks, you run the risk of "burnout." Even Jesus took breaks from his busy schedule to go off to a quiet place for solitude and prayer. Can our agenda be any more

important than our Lord's? Both you and your students need to take a break once in a while. Without them, the quality of work goes down, lethargy increases, and resentment builds. By wisely utilizing breaks, you are teaching your children a lesson that our society is not: we all need to slow down.

—Breaks should not disrupt the flow of your class. If you and your students are "on a roll," keep going. Don't take a break just for the sake of taking one. Be sure your breaks are well timed and effective.

Words to Remember

Attention span: Most of us only have the capability to pay attention to any one thing for so long before we get restless or distracted. In our highly technological age, we are bombarded with so much stimuli that our attention spans are decreasing. Children especially have very short attention spans and are easily distracted. As a catechist, you need to figure out ways of keeping your students' attention.

Solitude: How often do you get to be alone? How often do your students get to have some quiet time alone? We are almost always surrounded by other people and by noise and activity. One of the finest breaks you can provide for children is the experience of solitude. Solitude is the experience of being alone with your thoughts. Solitude can be achieved in the classroom by turning off the lights, lighting a candle, putting on some quiet music, and asking students to put their heads down and think about their day: the good, the not so good, the painful, and the joyful.

Sacred space: Closely related to the notion of solitude is the concept of *sacred space.* Many catechists allow children to find a spot anywhere in the classroom (at their desk, at the window, on the floor, under a table, etc.) that they can call their own. This space is referred to as *sacred* because it belongs to that child only and will be a space where he or she can experience solitude. Often, it is helpful to tell children to go to their sacred space to reflect on a story or question that you will be covering or just completed covering in class. If you are lucky enough, sacred space can also be utilized outside of the classroom (with the DRE's permission of course). Perhaps you have a chapel, a church, or an outdoor space that could be utilized. These sacred spaces provide some much needed solitude for children as they take an occasional break from the more cognitive pursuits of the lesson.

Troubleshooting

If you know anything about football, you may know that most quarterbacks receive the play they are about to run from the coach on the sideline, go over it in the huddle, and then execute it. Occasionally, however, the quarterback may look up right before he gets the ball and see a defensive lineup he did not expect to see. When this occurs, the quarterback calls an *audible,* which means that he changes the plan for the next play and calls it out to his teammates.

As a catechist, you are the quarterback of your class. Occasionally, you may look up at your class and notice something that you didn't expect to see (perhaps children who are sad because of an event in the news, etc.). Because of this, you may realize that your original play may not work. You need to call an audible. In other words, you need to be able to change your plan by providing your students with some kind of break or change of pace. It is helpful to have a favorite activity (perhaps a game or a prayer format) that you can go to on a moment's notice to keep your lesson from going over like a lead balloon.

● ●

Catechetical Dos and Don'ts

Do...
- be aware of your students' attention spans
- have breaks built into your lessons
- make your breaks educational/formational
- use prayer as a break

Don't...
- ignore the importance of breaks

- allow chaos or confusion
- disrupt the flow of your lesson
- ignore the importance of solitude

Catechist Quote

"I recall a particularly challenging day with a class of eighth graders. It was obvious that the students had other things on their mind which prevented them from being totally present and attentive. I told the class to shut their books and asked them, 'What's going on?' Well, that's all it took. Apparently, an incident had occurred at their school with a classmate who wasn't in our confirmation class but whom everyone knew. For the next fifteen minutes I let them talk about it as a group, sharing their feelings and opinions. The ensuing discussion had absolutely nothing to do with the lesson, or confirmation for that matter, but when we finally did return to the lesson, they were more attentive and responsive. As a result, I began to include a break time in every lesson in order to talk about what was going on in their lives; a reality session as they termed it. It has proven to be a wonderful, refreshing addition to the schedule—most appreciated by the students and catechist alike!"

—Todd Williamson (Eighth Grade Confirmation Preparation)

A Prayer for Catechists

"Come with me to an out-of-the-way place and rest a little" (Mk 6:31). Jesus, with these words, you showed your disciples how important it was to take a break from your work and focus on the reenergizing power of the spirit in prayer. Time and again, you went off into the wilderness to pray and experience solitude. If you were able to take a break from your ministry, then I should be able to do the same! Help me to trust that taking a break from my lessons can help both me and my students to refocus and reenergize so that we can return to our work with renewed vigor and enthusiasm for your Word. Amen.

Chapter Fourteen

Power Tools: Using AV Equipment

"We never needed any of these fancy, new-fangled tools. We did everything by hand! You guys today have got it easy…" These are the kinds of comments you hear when you attempt to use power tools in front of someone from the "old school." The truth is, things have really changed in the world of home repair. Today, power tools are available to drive a nail, sink a screw, sand a piece of wood, drill a hole, or even paint a wall. The trick, of course, is to make sure that you know how to use the power tools properly so that they really do complete your repairs in less time with greater efficiency. While power tools have changed the world of home repairs, one thing has not changed: the work needs to be done with care for detail and commitment to quality.

Power Tools for the Classroom

I recall one day when I was teaching religion in a high school, I went to pick up the VCR/TV from the librarian. As I entered the AV room, I was met with a flurry of activity that would have made Grand Central Station look deserted! Students were assisting the librarian in getting TV/VCRs, tape players, slide machines, overhead projectors, and a variety of other machines ready for delivery to classrooms. The librarian took a deep breath, looked over at me and said, "What did Thomas Aquinas and St. Augustine do without AV equipment?"

It's true that for centuries our most celebrated teachers accomplished great things without the assistance of an ounce of electricity! By the same token, they used whatever was state of the art for their day. As literacy became more and more widespread, the written word came to be just as crucial as the spoken word that once seemed sufficient. The fact is, today we live in an age of technology. Our children are learning to use computers in the primary grades the way many of us once learned to finger through Dick and Jane books. They are accustomed to being entertained by video images and audio sounds for the majority of their day. It only makes sense that religious education attempt to utilize the tools that are available today to reach our children in the most effective manner. Let's take a look at how we can most effectively use AV resources in our classrooms to enhance our lessons.

Tips on Using AV Equipment

Jesus used the state-of-the-art media of his day: the oral proclamation! Jesus was a master of the spoken word, using parables and discourses to leave his audiences spellbound. In addition, he engaged peoples' visual senses by performing signs and miracles that captured their imaginations and invited them to consider the possibility of new life. Our goal as catechists is to utilize AV equipment in the same manner, in an effort to engage our audiences and stimulate their imaginations to consider endless possibilities. As we approach the world of AV resources, let's keep the following tips in mind.

1. *Decide on the most effective medium for your lesson.* Always go back to your goals and objectives for the lesson. Using AV equipment must fit in with these if it is to be effective. If your goals call for engaging students in an experience of sharing and articulating, then it may not be the right time to show a video that will make them passive. Remember that any AV resource is a tool to help you achieve a goal. One does not use a power drill to sand a piece of wood! Be sure your selection of AV equipment will help you achieve your lesson's goals and objectives.

2. *Familiarize yourself with the equipment.* Let's face it, some AV equipment can be intimidating. If we do not use VCRs, slide projectors, and CD players much at home, we will find these devices foreign. Be sure to take the time to look over the equipment you are going to use to familiarize yourself with

its features and directions for use.

3. ***Do a test run on your presentation.*** Part of familiarizing yourself with the equipment is testing all of the settings. How do you work the volume, brightness, play, stop, pause, etc.? I find it helpful to place a bright sticker on the buttons I need to use in order to find them quickly during the lesson. In addition, running a test on the equipment will help you make sure all of the "bugs" have been worked out.

4. ***Don't trust AV equipment just because it's AV equipment.*** We sometimes have a tendency to relax when AV equipment is being used in our classes because as a society, we have developed such a blind trust for technology. We assume that it is going to work just because it is a product of modern technology. Don't fall into this trap. Numerous problems arise in the classroom when using AV equipment because teachers trust their equipment so implicitly that they don't think it necessary to check it out ahead of time.

5. ***Preview all of your materials.*** Aside from your equipment, be sure to preview anything you are showing on a VCR or overhead projector or are playing on a cassette or CD player. Your video tape may not be good quality. Your transparency may be in upside down or may contain spelling mistakes. Your tape or CD may not be the right one. The bottom line is, don't spend so much time inspecting the equipment that you ignore the material you will be placing into it.

6. ***Have your tapes or CDs forwarded to the correct place.*** Few things can frustrate a catechist more than attempting to play a video, CD, or tape and finding that the tape or CD is forwarded to the wrong spot. The time it takes to locate the correct space can seem like an eternity and can result in loss a of control of your class. It is important to have your tapes and CDs lined up to begin at the precise moment you press "play."

7. ***Practice shutting off equipment.*** This may sound strange, but the inability to turn *off* equipment can be just as frustrating to your lesson as the inability to turn on equipment. The mood you had hoped to set by showing a video clip or playing a

song may be thoroughly lost by what follows on the tape or CD or by the static that erupts because you can't find the "stop" button. It is always a good idea to slowly fade the "volume" before pressing "stop" on any piece of equipment. I've seen more prayerful moods destroyed by catechists who hit the "stop" button in the middle of a song or video clip because it was time to move on. The resulting abrupt silence can be disconcerting to a class that was being engaged by the viewing or listening.

8. *AV equipment is a means to an end, not an end in and of itself.* Recall that AV resources are a tool to assist you in achieving the goals and objectives of your lesson. For that reason, it is important to provide your students with an introduction to anything they are about to see or hear. Always provide an introduction and overview to whatever videos, tapes, or CDs you are about to play. Likewise, give your students something to focus on while any tape or CD is being played so that they do not merely become passive. Instruct your students to pay attention to certain details and have them jot down notes on a worksheet as they watch or listen. When the viewing or listening is over, always help the children process what they have seen or heard by integrating it into the lesson.

Warning!

—AV equipment can be the catechist's best friend and worst enemy. When prepared for and used properly, AV equipment can enhance the effectiveness of your lesson. However, the reliance on powers beyond your control can result in glitches that can ruin your lesson. There is always a risk involved whenever using AV equipment. Be prepared for whatever may go wrong and have a backup plan ready.

—Children have high expectations of AV presentations and can easily be bored if it is less than quality. Showing a filmstrip or even a "video-strip" will seem as ancient to your students as a message chiseled out on a tablet. Likewise, be careful to show videos and play music that is contemporary. Showing a video clip or playing a song you enjoyed from the sixties or seventies will be comic to children of today's world. Because of the rapid rate of technological progress, it doesn't take very long for something to go out of style.

Words to Remember

VCR: Today, the video cassette recorder is as common in most homes as a transistor radio once was. Most children know how to operate a VCR. Because of this, you may want to enlist the assistance of a reliable student in operating the VCR so that you are free to continue paying attention to the rest of the class. A VCR is perhaps the most common tool used in the classroom today. Numerous quality videos are available for use in religious education. Likewise, it is easy for catechists to record contemporary TV programs or news clips for use in the class to connect the lesson to current events.

Projection TV: Many religious education programs are lucky enough to have access to a projection TV which allows you to show a video or a TV program to a larger group of students on a large screen as though you were showing a movie. A projection TV simply projects the image onto a large screen for viewing by a larger audience.

Overhead projector: An overhead projector is basically an electronic chalkboard. Catechists can effectively utilize transparencies to illustrate or outline important points for a lesson without ever having to turn your back on your class to write on the board. Children are easily engaged by use of an overhead because the lights go off and their focus is easily fixed on the large bright image. Be aware of the need to prepare transparencies ahead of time and always have an extra bulb on hand in case one burns out.

CD/cassette player: Today, CDs have replaced vinyl records and are rapidly replacing even cassette tapes. A CD is a compact disc that plays music by result of laser instead of a needle or tape heads. The clarity of a CD is unsurpassed and can provide some excellent sounds for your classroom prayer experiences. Audio cassettes continue to be reliable and less expensive than CDs. Both CD and audio cassette players work much the same way with simple "on/off," "play," "pause," "forward," "rewind," and "stop" buttons. With CDs it is easier to locate a song on the disc because of the track selection feature.

Troubleshooting

When showing a video, you may find the picture to be slightly distorted. Be sure you learn how to utilize the tracking feature to bring greater clarity to your picture.

—Other glitches may pop up when using AV equipment. Make sure you know who you can call on (DRE, maintenance person, colleague, reliable student, etc.) to come to the rescue without having to leave your class.

—Check on the visibility and audibility of your presentation. Nothing is worse than starting a video, tape, or CD, only to realize that a majority of your class cannot see or hear it. Part of your preparation should be to make sure that every seat in the "house" is good.

—Most problems using AV equipment can easily be avoided with proper preparation. Power buttons, cords, volume switches, etc., rarely cause trouble unless we are using them improperly. Minimize these problems by doing your homework before class begins.

• •

Catechetical Dos and Don'ts

Do...
• familiarize yourself with equipment
• prepare by doing a trial run
• employ a variety of AV resources
• preview/introduce AV presentations
• integrate AVs into your lesson

•have a backup plan

Don't...
•blindly trust technology
•proceed without proper setup
•put too much emphasis on AVs
•substitute AVs for human interaction
•be intimidated by AVs
•use AVs as a "way out" of teaching

• •

Catechist Quote

"My seventh graders once felt as though the videos I was show-ing them were too 'juvenile.' I solicited suggestions and lo and behold, Jim Carrey's *The Mask* was a popular choice. Needless to say, I was hesitant. The movie contained a love interest and a cer-tain amount of violence. A show of hands revealed that most stu-dents had already seen it. Since I had already seen it, I recalled that the key to the movie was that the mask is thrown away and the main character realizes that he does not need to pretend to be someone else. I had just been trying to teach my seventh graders how important it was to know themselves and take responsibili-ty for being a good Catholic. We were learning about peer pres-sure and the roles played during adolescence. In the end, I decid-ed to show the movie. We discussed the story *before* we watched it and talked about why the mask was thrown away. They dis-cussed the various 'masks' that they wore and how they could help or hurt. After viewing the movie, we actually made masks. I found it was important to take a movie they liked and draw out an important message. I think they were surprised to see how flexible I could be and even more surprised that they could learn something religious from a 'silly' movie!"

—Gregoria Vega-Byrnes
(Eighth Grade Confirmation Preparation)

A Prayer for Catechists

Jesus, you were a carpenter. You used the best tools that were available to you to carve, saw, sand, and nail. In your ministry, you also used the best tools available to you: parables, proclamations, discourses, signs, miracles, and wonders. By using these tools, you were able to engage your audience and leave them spellbound. Today, there are so many tools available to use in preaching your Word: videos, CDs, cassettes, overhead projectors, etc. Help me to best utilize audiovisual tools in my teaching so that I may capture the imagination of my students and bring the power of your Word to life. Amen.

Chapter Fifteen

The Scraper: Using Questions to Get Beneath the Surface

When my wife and I bought our first house, we were impressed mainly with its potential. It was a small, cute little house and as we toured it the first time, we saw many possibilities for decorating. After we moved in, the work began. Every room and every wall had to be painted or wallpapered. Off with the green, pink, and brown that covered the walls and hid their potential beauty. Easier said than done! For whatever reason, the previous owner had decided to glue most of the wallpaper on. What I thought was going to be an easy "peeling off" job became a project for my scraper. Bit by bit, I scraped off the old wallpaper which stubbornly held onto the wall. It took a great deal of effort, but eventually, I was able to get down to the smooth natural surface of the wall and begin the fun task of putting up the new wallpaper. The result was tremendous—the little house that we thought had so much potential lived up to our dream!

Uncovering Their Potential

The children we teach are so much like the walls in my little house—so full of potential. We just need to know how to get beneath the surface or exterior that covers that potential. As teachers, one of the most effective ways we do this is by using the tool of asking questions.

Jesus was, of course, a master at this. Often in the gospels, we see Jesus utilizing questions to challenge his followers and stimulate their thinking: "Who do *you* say that I am? What is the inscription on this coin? What did you go out to the desert to see? Didn't you know that I had to be in my Father's house? Is it easier to say 'Your sins are forgiven you' or 'Get up and walk'? Do you think you can make the guests at a wedding party go without food as long as the bridegroom is with them? In your opinion, which of these acted like a neighbor toward the man attacked by the robbers?" And the list goes on.

Jesus knew that asking questions was a valuable tool that helped to get beneath the surface and unleash the potential that was there. As catechists, we too need to utilize questions in our classroom so that we may get beneath the surface of our students and tap the rich potential that lies inside of them.

Tips on Asking Questions

One of Jesus' most famous sayings refers to the act of asking a question: "Ask, and you shall receive." Another famous anonymous saying tells us that "He who asks questions cannot avoid the answers." I have come to believe that our task as catechists is not so much to provide answers for our students, but to teach them to ask the right questions in their lives, knowing that when they ask, they shall receive. Let's take a look at the proper use of questions in the classroom.

1. *Phrase your questions in a simple, straightforward way.* Children will not answer a question if they are not sure what you are asking. Avoid complicated questions that turn and twist so much that students can't figure out what you're really looking for. Keep the question short and to the point.

2. *Keep your questions open-ended.* Avoid asking questions that will result in a yes or no response. An open-ended question is one that invites the student to dig a little deeper and express some thoughts, insights, and opinions of their own. For example, instead of asking, "Did Jesus ever show any feelings or emotions?" you could ask, "When were some times that Jesus showed feelings or emotions?"

3. *Don't answer your own questions.* All too often, catechists panic when no hands go up to answer a question. To save face, they answer the question themselves and then move on. Remember our chapter on the spotlight? When you ask a

question, you have placed the focus on the students. Keep it there. Be patient. Give the children time to think. If they're having trouble answering, try rephrasing the question.

4. *Always repeat a question.* Asking a question once is never enough. Get in the habit of asking a question, pausing, and then asking the question again in exactly the same way. Do this even if a hand shoots up after the first time. Quite often, the same child is quick to raise their hand while it may take some students just a little longer to refine their answer. By pausing and repeating the question, you give these students an opportunity to jump in.

5. *Move around the room and make eye contact.* As you ask and repeat a question, move around the room and make eye contact with students. This is a way of communicating to them that you expect an answer and will patiently wait until you get one.

6. *Ask a question of the whole class first.* Whenever you ask a question, direct it to the whole class first. Don't single out a student and put them on the spot. Occasionally you may need to single out someone whose attention is wavering, but the whole class should have the opportunity to respond. If you single out one child, the rest of the class will relax thinking that they're off the hook.

7. *Plan your questions ahead of time.* The questions you ask should be well thought out and planned ahead of time so that they fit in as tools that will move your lesson along in the right direction. If you do not plan your questions, you run the risk of going blank or asking poor questions that will grind your lesson to a halt. Write out your questions and evaluate their quality. Shorten and rephrase them until you feel they will achieve their goal most effectively.

8. *Give feedback to students when they respond to questions.* Children react to affirmation. If a child answers a question and you simply take the answer and go somewhere with it, they will feel ignored or unappreciated. Children participate more if they feel you are interested in them and in what they have to say. Be sure to tell students, "That's excellent!" or "That's a very good point you make." Even if a student

answers incorrectly, do not embarrass them by saying, "No, you're wrong." Instead, say something like, "Nice try...let's see if someone can help you."

Warning!
Keep in mind the old saying, "Be careful what you ask for, you just may get it." Asking children questions opens up a whole universe of possible answers, some of which may truly be out of this world! Remember that children can say the darnedest things and will ask the darnedest things as well. Be prepared for the unexpected. Don't panic. Most often, these situations will turn out to be lighthearted, such as the time a catechist was discussing the story of Jesus talking to the Pharisees about paying taxes. As she passed a quarter around asking students what Jesus said about the inscription, a little girl replied, "Hey, where's Caesar's face?" By the same token, however, children's comments, questions, or responses may leave you stumped or flabbergasted. If it's appropriate and worthwhile, probe further. If not, calmly deflect the comment or question and say, "We'll talk more about that some other time."

Words to Remember

I have come to categorize the various types of questions teachers ask into two basic categories: impersonal and personal. Each of these categories can be further broken down into two smaller categories. Like peeling away layers of an onion, each category delves deeper into the heart of the responder. The four I's, as I refer to them, describe the type of answer the questioner is looking for.

IMPERSONAL

Informational: A question in this category is just skimming the surface and is very nonthreatening; a great way to begin a discussion. An example would be, "What is another name for

Jesus' Sermon on the Mount?" The answer is strictly informational: "the Beatitudes."

Implicational: Questions used in this category go beneath the surface somewhat and attempt to arrive at the significance of the information being discussed. An example would be, "What is Jesus trying to tell us in the Beatitudes?" At this point, the response still does not necessarily reflect any personal information.

PERSONAL

Individual: A question from this category delves into the thoughts, opinions, and feelings of the individual responding. Obviously, this type of question can be more threatening because more is being revealed. On the other hand, they can be so much more meaningful and enjoyable. An example would be, "How can *you* try to live out the Beatitudes in your life?"

Ideological: The dictionary defines ideological as "fanciful or visionary speculation." An ideological question invites students to speculate. Such questions expect no clear cut answer but challenge students to grapple with issues that are beyond their ability to totally grasp. An example of this may be, "What do you think the world would look like if everyone followed the Beatitudes?" When any of us responds on this level, we are revealing our most personal selves—our dreams!

Troubleshooting

Few things can make a class more silent than a question asked by a teacher. Rather than grow nervous about the silence, relish the fact that you have engaged the students. The silence reflects the fact that they are thinking. Be patient, repeat the question, rephrase it if necessary, but resist the temptation to answer it yourself. Sooner or later an answer will come. Ask and you shall receive!

• •

Catechetical Dos and Don'ts

Do...
•prepare your questions

- keep your questions simple
- ask open-ended questions
- repeat your question
- be patient for a response
- affirm student responses

Don't...
- answer your own questions
- use questions to embarrass a child
- panic when no one answers
- only ask informational questions
- be satisfied with only one answer
- be afraid to reply "I don't know but I'll find out" to student questions

Catechist Quote

"Whenever I ask a question, I have found it helpful to have what we call 'Think Time,' a short period during which no hands go up until we've had a chance to formulate our thoughts. Likewise, I find it helpful in most lessons to ask, 'What's the issue?' For example, when Jesus cured the lepers, was it just about showing power to cure or was the issue how Jesus continuously went beyond the boundaries of society? Something else I like to do is to place 'wisdom' questions on our walls: 'When am I in God's presence? When do I see Jesus? What is Holy Ground?' When we discuss these, I also find it effective to invite the children to compose their own wisdom questions. Questions are indeed like a scraper. Some scraping needs to be done with an extra gentle touch, especially when we're right near the original masterpiece! Finally, I need a scraper for myself at times. I ask Jesus to help me scrape away my own uncertainties about my ability to help the children."

—Barb McMillin (Fifth grade)

A Prayer for Catechists

Jesus, you said, "Ask and you shall receive." Help me to know *what* to ask. Help me to ask questions of my students that will get beneath the surface and delve into their hearts so that their true potential may be unlocked and the power of your spirit unleashed. As if scraping away old paint or wallpaper, help me to use questions to reveal the true beauty of each child and to teach them to ask the right questions of life so that its mysteries will slowly and gradually be revealed to them. May they come to recognize time and again that *you* are the answer they are seeking. Amen.

Chapter Sixteen

Apprenticeship: Learning by Doing

My father was a pharmacist and worked in the family drugstore from 9 AM to 9 PM. The only tools I ever saw him use were a mortar and pestle! I never saw him paint, hammer, saw, or drill. Needless to say, I was apprenticed in the ways of running a retail pharmacy, *not* in the ways of home repairs. Both worlds collided, however, when our family business was forced to move into a new storefront that was badly in need of redecorating and repairs. I quickly volunteered to paint, wallpaper, and lay in a new floor. Only one problem stood in the way—I didn't know how to do any of these things! Luckily for me, my brother-in-law was quite handy with tools and home repairs and stepped forward to lend his expertise. Over the next few weeks, I learned more about home repairs than I had previously learned during my entire life because I was apprenticed to someone who had been there before and knew how to show me the way. From laying down tiles to assembling store fixtures, my brother-in-law provided me with numerous opportunities to try things I had never done before and, in doing so, learn some tricks of the trade.

It's All in the Doing

An ancient proverb says that to know, but not to do, is really not to know. As a catechist, we can attend all kinds of workshops and read all kinds of books (like this one!) and come to the conclusion that we really know how to be an effective catechist. However, the only real teacher in life is experience. It is in the *doing* of catechesis that we grow and develop in our ministry. By the same token, it is only when our students become involved in doing the work of the gospel that they truly learn the gospel. It is through doing and reflecting upon our experience that we come to realize that the Lord is indeed moving in our midst. Let's take a look at how we as catechists can learn by doing and how we in turn can teach more effectively.

Tips on Apprenticing

FOR OURSELVES

1. *Try new things.* A contemporary definition of insanity is to do the same thing over and over again while expecting different results. If we are dissatisfied with the effectiveness of our lessons and would like to achieve different results, we cannot continue to do the same thing every time we teach! Part of being an apprentice is the opportunity to try out new skills under the supervision of a mentor. Think of yourself as an apprentice (no matter how long you've been teaching), eager to try out something new in your class in hopes of bringing about new results.

2. *Get a coach.* A coach, a mentor, a master catechist—call it what you want, but every apprentice needs a teacher. Whether it be your DRE, a colleague catechist, a parent, or a teacher you once had, maintain communication with your coach so that he or she can provide you with the insight you need to hone your skills and continue acquiring new ones. Seek out veteran catechists who have a whole trunk load of skills and ideas that you would love to implement in your class. By the same token, veteran catechists should seek out new catechists to see what kinds of fresh, creative, and energetic ideas they are bringing to the classroom. Apprenticeship can and should go both ways!

3. *Accept new challenges.* When I agreed to remodel that new storefront of my dad's pharmacy, I was accepting a challenge

to do something I did not really know how to do but desperately wanted to learn. As a catechist, don't be afraid of challenges your DRE sends your way. You may be asked to take on a new subject, a new age group, or become a leader of prayer or liturgical minister for children's liturgies. Don't shy away from these challenges. Accept them and find a coach that will assist you in developing in this new area you are venturing into.

4. *Learn from your mistakes.* Apprentices make mistakes, and so will you. The difference between an effective catechist and one who is not is the ability to learn from those mistakes. If things go wrong in your class, don't say, "Never again!" Instead, ask yourself, "How will I do this differently next time?" because there *will* be a next time. Nothing is learned from a mistake that is swept under the carpet.

In my own experience, as a young catechist, I once led a prayer service for teens that resulted in a young man crying in front of everyone. I was embarrassed for him and told everyone we would take a break while I led him out of the room to compose himself. The associate pastor (my coach) who was present at the time later told me that I had no reason to lead that young man out of the room. His tears were his prayer. I could have comforted him and affirmed his sharing of emotion. I felt terrible that I communicated to this young man that crying was wrong. Instead of staying away from emotional prayer experiences, I vowed to change the way I reacted to tears.

Since that time, I have had many people, young and old, cry in the presence of others while at prayer. I have learned to quietly comfort them, often just by placing a hand on their shoulder, and thank them for sharing their tears with the group. I believe that from my mistake, I learned to become a better catechist and have helped others to express themselves in whatever way the spirit moves them.

FOR OUR STUDENTS

1. *Become a coach.* As a catechist, you need to begin seeing yourself as a coach or mentor and your students as appren-

tices. Your job is to begin showing them how to use the skills they will need to succeed in life as a Christian. A good coach lets the players play the game. A good catechist learns how to teach from the sidelines, allowing students to put skills and ideas to work while offering them guidance and support.

2. *Let go.* As catechists, we sometimes think that if something is going to get done, we have to do it ourselves. Wrong! The best catechists know how to share the work with their students and, in doing so, make them apprentices. Show students how to take attendance, write on the board for you, distribute and collect books and papers, lead prayer, and even lead discussion. Your students are not sponges waiting to soak up your wisdom. They are apprentices, waiting to be shown how to use the skills you were once taught.

3. *Think of John the Baptist.* Whenever I start to do too much by myself, I try to remind myself of John the Baptist who said, "Now I must decrease and He must increase" (Jn 3:30). This is the prayer of a mentor or coach. John knew when it was time for him to step aside and allow Jesus to reach his potential. As catechists, we too need to step aside and allow our children to reach their potential by allowing them to do the work of the gospel while we coach them.

4. *Think laboratory and field trips.* A laboratory is a place where experiments are conducted. Our classrooms are just that, laboratories where we experiment with the gospel message of Jesus and test it out before putting it into practice in the real world. Our lessons should be seen as experiments in Christianity and our students as apprentices who are, for the first time, testing the hypotheses of their predecessors under our supervision. By the same token, the best "laboratory" experiments are those that are tested in the real world. Employing this "field trip" theory in your classroom means preparing your lessons with a focus on applying new knowledge and skills in real life situations. At times, you will actually be able to arrange field trips for your class, such as doing a service project which calls for the principles of charity and humility. You might also give assignments that require stu-

dents to test out or apply principles taught in class. For example, if you are talking about love of enemies or turning the other cheek, give your students an assignment that will require them to perform some action that applies these principles. Later, discuss the successes and failures that they encountered.

Warning!

A good coach, teacher, or mentor knows not to overwhelm their apprentice. It is one thing to offer new opportunities and challenges to students and another thing to toss them in where they will be "in over their head." For example, we may want to apprentice our children in the art of expressing their faith in front of others. That does not mean that we have to force children to stand in front of the class and bare their souls. Apprenticeship must be incremental. Begin small and move on to larger challenges little by little, coaching your students along the way.

Words to Remember

Mentor: The word *mentor* is the name of a mythical character in *The Odyssey* who was a very wise guardian. We too are called to be "wise guardians" or guides to our children. The more trust we place in our students, the more trust they develop in us. The mentor / apprentice relationship is based on and thrives upon this mutual trust.

Apprentice: The dictionary tells us that an apprentice is any beginner or learner who is bound to another for a fixed period of time in order to learn a trade, skill, or business. While this sounds formal, it really does apply. Our children *are* beginners, but we must recall that we were and still are as well. We *are* bound to one another for a fixed period of time. So we should use this time to hand on both the knowledge and skills that were handed on to us.

Troubleshooting

Teaching apprentices requires great patience. Sometimes apprentices make mistakes. A good coach or mentor knows how to offer correction without tearing someone down. If you place responsibility in the hands of one of your students and are let down, take a deep breath and handle the situation calmly, not sarcastically. Never criticize publicly. Rather, take your apprentice aside and offer correction and advice privately, all the while encouraging your student to begin asking, "How will I do this differently next time?" because there *will* be a next time!

• •

Catechetical Dos and Don'ts

Do...
• trust and let go
• try new things
• develop a list of tasks students can do
• get yourself a coach or mentor
• raise your own standards

Don't...
• try to do it all by yourself
• run from your mistakes
• overwhelm your apprentices
• avoid challenges
• lose your patience

• •

Catechist Quote

"I have found that the best way to encourage our 'apprentices' to try new things is to first create an atmosphere of trust and respect. It takes time—weeks, maybe even months—but once they know that it is safe to be themselves, students will risk making mistakes and they will try new things. The same is true for teachers! I remember hearing a teacher yell, 'Who spilled that milk? I want to know right now and we won't go home until I find out!' I was just walking past the room but the anger in the tone of voice filled me with fear. As an adult, *I* wouldn't have admitted to spilling the milk for fear of what might be done to me! In that type of atmosphere, one will only do what is safe, what is tried and true. If we feel threatened, we will never risk trying something new. We should help our students look upon a mistake as a mis-take: they reached for something and missed! The important thing is that they *did* reach for something! In this type of environment, students and teachers will feel safe to reach for new things. They will become more actively involved in the lesson. Choose a mentor. At the same time, be a mentor who removes the fear from trying new things!"

—Ken Koll (DRE)

A Prayer for Catechists

St. Paul said, "I received from the Lord what I handed unto you..." as he wrote to the Corinthians about the Lord's Supper. Paul was apprenticed ("I received...") and was now apprenticing ("what I handed unto you..."). Thank you, Lord, for those coaches, teachers, and mentors who apprenticed and continue to apprentice me as I struggle to acquire the knowledge and skills needed to live the gospel. Help me, in turn, Lord, to apprentice my students, to hand unto them that which I have received so that they may also become your disciples and live out the good news of the Kingdom of God. Amen.

Conclusion

Looking for Results

Throughout this work, I have been making comparisons between home repair tools and the tools needed for catechesis. Many similarities exist, however, there is one major difference. Typically, when we complete some home repairs, we can stand back and look at the final outcome, taking satisfaction in the tangible results. As a catechist, our results will be much less tangible. How does one know when a life has been touched, a soul has been stirred, or a spirit aroused? Most often you will not know the extent to which your lesson and your presence have been effective.

When I was a high school teacher, a former student came back to see me some five years after graduation. He thanked me for a particular class session I taught him when he was a student, saying that it really came in handy now that he was in college and in the workplace. I went home knowing that I had a good day some five or six years ago! Many of us will never know what effect we have had on our students. For this reason, it is all the more crucial to focus on acquiring the tools needed to be an effective catechist, for the more refined our skills, the more sensitive we will be to the effects of our lessons. The more specific we are about our own expectations of the class, the more specific the results will be.

Just how much we may have touched the lives of our students, we may never know. But with the proper tools for teaching, we will leave our classes knowing that, in some way, the

Word of God *has* touched their lives. In the end, we must realize that we are simply a tool in the hand of God who alone is Teacher and Lord.

Suggested Resources
for Catechist Enrichment

All of the following resources are available from Twenty-Third Publications, P.O. Box 180, Mystic, CT 06355, 1–800–321–0411.

Video Programs

Empowering the Catechist
Skills and Techniques for Effective Teaching
Joseph Paprocki
This video series is a great motivator. Topics include the importance of catechetical ministry, lesson planning, a positive environment, motivating students, discipline, and prayer. Especially convenient to use in parishes where professional training is not available. Comes with a leader's guide and a free copy of *Creative Catechist*. Six 30-minute sessions, $99.00.

Enriching the Catechist
Brennan Hill and William Madges
This six-part video program will help catechists add richness and theological continuity to their religious education programs. Two well-known theologians and a diverse team of religious educators identify fundamental doctrines of the Catholic faith and issues of theological importance. Appropriate for teachers of all grade levels. Six 30-minute sessions, $99.00.

Books

Prayer Services for Catechist and Teacher Meetings
Gwen Costello
This is a wonderful resource for DREs and principals to use with catechists and teachers. The themes relate to teacher interests and concerns. Since an important, even essential aspect of Christian proclamation is prayer, these 30 services offer participants an opportunity to pray together and to grow in the habit of prayer. Each is a complete prayer experience that also teaches valuable faith lessons and can be used for meetings during the school year and specifically for the beginning of a new teaching year, All

Saints, Thanksgiving, Advent, Christmas, Lent, Easter, Pentecost, and Ordinary Time. $12.95.

Creative Catechist: A Comprehensive, Illustrated Guide for Training Religion Teachers
Janaan Manternach and Carl Pfeifer
This is an ideal book both for in-service and pre-service teacher training. Catechists will find practical help here with lesson planning, discipline, classroom techniques, student motivation and grading, use of media to enrich lessons, guides to class prayer——all the elements that enable a religion teacher to become a creative catechist. $12.95.

Discipline Made Easy: Positive Tips and Techniques for Religion Teachers
Kathleen Mary Glavich, SND
This informative and practical book offers hundreds of tested techniques to provide encouragement to new volunteer catechists and wise insight to veterans. An excellent guide for religion teachers at any grade level. $7.95.

Jesus, I'm a Teacher Too
Guidance and Inspiration from the Gospels
Melannie Svoboda, SND
Whether used for personal or group reflection and prayer, this book will help religion teachers learn from St. Mark's Jesus what it means to be a dedicated teacher. The author reveals the compassion and gifts of Jesus, the master teacher. Insights and inspiration abound. $9.95.

Teaching Is Like...Peeling Back Eggshells
Melannie Svoboda, SND
The author suggests that a teacher is like a farmer helping young chicks to hatch by gently peeling back a portion of the eggshell so as to ease the birth (of new ideas for students). Warm and witty, these fifty reflections of an outstanding teacher will give catechists the boost they need to continue the important task of being effective, enthusiastic teachers. $7.95.

Psalm Services for Group Prayer
William Cleary
The ancient psalms of David form the basis for half the prayer services in this book. The other half features original psalms by the author. Services are approximately 5–8 minutes in length, encourage involvement, and offer a variety of themes for use in any parish gathering. Inspirational for use during liturgical seasons as well as for key moments in catechists' lives. $12.95.

A Way of the Cross for Religion Teachers
Gwen Costello
At each stop on Jesus' way to Calvary, catechists are given insights into the challenges and trials of their ministry through this unique devotional booklet. It's ideal for teacher meetings during Lent and also for personal prayer. $1.95.

A Teacher's Prayerbook: To Know and Love Your Students
Ginger Farry
Written by a full-time teacher who often brings her students to God, this delightful book contains prayer poems for and about students. These prayers chronicle the good and bad days, the joys and disappointments in the life of a teacher. Each prayer is followed by a brief reflection or questions for teachers to ponder in relation to their own students. $4.95.

Five Dynamic Dimensions for Effective Teaching
Kevin Treston
This contemporary book describes five important aspects of a teacher's vocation: integrity, wisdom, generativity, learning, and justice. The author encourages teachers to foster these qualities so as to be learning companions with students on the journey of life and faith. A must read for those who want to deepen their understanding of the teaching vocation. $9.95.

Of Related Interest

Discipline Made Easy
Positive Tips and Techniques for Religion Teachers
Sr. Kathleen Glavich
Here the author provides hundreds of tested techniques to give encouragement to volunteer catechists and wise insights to veterans.
ISBN: 0-89622-598-4, 112 pp, $7.95

Teaching Is Like...
Peeling Back Eggshells
Melannie Svoboda
The author suggests that a teacher is like a farmer who helps young chicks to hatch by gently peeling back a portion of the eggshell so as to ease their birth (of new ideas for students). Warm and witty, these 50 reflections of an outstanding teacher will give catechists the boost they need to continue the important task of being an effective, enthusiastic teacher.
ISBN: 0-89622-613-1, 120 pp, $7.95

Seven Steps to Great Religion Classes
Gwen Costello and Joe Paprocki
The authors take you step by step through seven important elements of a "great religion class": the qualities of a good catechist; the process of lesson planning; skills needed to create a positive environment; strategies for motivating children; techniques for maintaining and handling discipline; and skills in sharing and leading meaningful prayer experiences. Each chapter includes reflection and discussion questions, and a concluding prayer. An excellent resource for every catechist and religion teacher!
ISBN: 0-89622-934-3, 80 pp, $7.95

Empowering the Catechist
Skills and Techniques for Effective Teaching
Joe Paprocki
In this six-session video series, catechists learn invaluable skills such as how to prepare for the challenges of being a catechist, how to create a positive faith environment, and ways to prepare meaningful class prayer experiences. Comes with a free copy of Creative Catechist.
$99.00 (order A-84)

Available at religious bookstores or from:

XXIII **TWENTY-THIRD PUBLICATIONS**
P.O. Box 180 • Mystic, CT 06355

For a complete list of quality books and videos call:
1 - 8 0 0 - 3 2 1 - 0 4 1 1